LIFE FOR BEGINNERS

Almost all diseases are easier prevented than afterwards removed

James Lind 1752

*Originally human beings had no purpose, now they dream up a
purpose.   It is a one-man wrestling match. The human being
was a happy creature, but they created a hard world and
now struggle to break out of it.*

*In Nature there is life and death, and nature is joyful. In Human
Society there is life and death and people live in sorrow.*

Masanobu Fukuoka 1972

LIFE FOR BEGINNERS

Balance and Moderation

Anthony Smith

JUNIPERLAND PUBLICATIONS

Published by:

JUNIPERLAND PUBLICATIONS
The Station House
Wickenby
Lincoln
LN3 5AN

ISBN 0-9551914-0-8

Made and Printed in Great Britain

With Thanks

My wife Jennifer for her tolerance.

My daughter Sarah for her patience with her ignorant father with his haphazard computer skills.

The Open University.

Nick Cheffins for reawakening my academic side and then going out on a limb, when it wasn't necessary, in nurturing and supporting me in my efforts.

John Seddon without whom this project would possibly never have reached a conclusion.

Frontispiece

"FLUID MOZAIC"

by

Marjorie Smith

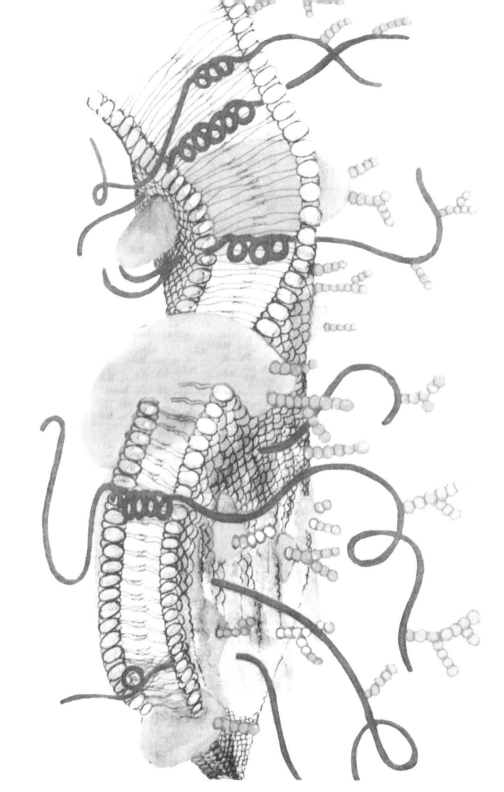

Contents

INTRODUCTION

Over the last 30 to 40 years there has been a huge change in Science and Technology. The result of this has led to a massive increase in scientific knowledge in relation to the working of cells, which all living organisms are made up of. No longer is the cell thought of as a water filled balloon with a few bits and pieces arbitrarily floating around in it. Each living cell is now known to be as organized and complex as a town or city and the various floating bits, known as organelles, are carrying out a large number of functions. There has been a vast increase in knowledge of Biochemistry, the role of what are now hundreds of hormones and the subject of Genetics. This rapid increase in knowledge of how the body works has also led to medical advances at an ever increasing pace, with the development of micro-surgery and less invasive procedures.

Much of this increase can be strongly accredited to the development of the microchip. This has led to an explosion in the development of electronic devices for use in a laboratory setting and allowed faster and greater insight and detection of biochemical reactions. The role and systematic structure of DNA has also been largely solved in much quicker time due to the electronic revolution. The age of the computer has brought great, great benefits and the Internet is probably mankind's greatest invention. The world has now got a wealth of knowledge readily available at its fingertips in a form which must have been pure fantasy only a short time ago. The computer now affects all aspects of life but, as with many inventions and developments, the balance is probably incorrect. The computer is almost certainly over-used and abused. It is attached to all manner of everyday items sometimes with little or no benefit and it appears that nothing can be developed without using it. I will admit to being something of a dinosaur regarding the computer. I grew up without the computer and often cannot see why it is used in some circumstances. Possibly, as a whole, we have never had it so good but, there are definitely aspects of life from the past which were done better than the present. We were probably healthier 40 years ago as we were more active with a higher level of general exercise. Think of the motor car. The present day habit of computerization means that whereas reliability has increased, when something goes wrong it is often less readily fixed. Perhaps it is no bad thing that repairs and maintenance are left these days to the appropriate engineers, but there are many older people about who happily used to do it themselves.

In general the medical profession are beyond reproach and their dedication must be admired. The aim of the medical profession is quite obviously to make ill people well again. Unfortunately, with the overwhelming work load general practitioners not surprisingly may have a somewhat narrow view and find themselves treating symptoms instead of the underlying cause of disease processes. There is little scope to practice preventative medicine and general practitioner training is light on dealing with life-style problems such as diet. Both doctors and dentists are not above criticism for being sanctimonious in their dealings with patients but fortunately this all too common trait in the dental profession is becoming less. There have been huge advances in medical knowledge, diagnosis and treatment but, there has also been an enormous increase in life-style related diseases which possibly neither doctors' or dentists' training prepared them for. Let us take the common complaint of hypertension. This has traditionally been treated with a range of prescription medications, sometimes producing side effects, which in turn requires even more medication. Would it not have been better, if the time was available, to do a thorough evaluation of the patient's life-style to elicit the probable cause of the hypertension and then see if appropriate action could be taken to reduce it without resorting to drug therapy. I am sure there are an increasing number of over-worked doctors about who feel this way, but are not in a position to do much about it.

So what about life-style. Returning to an earlier statement that we have never had it so good, let us look at present life. Many people now live in relatively new housing which is reasonably well insulated with no draughts, double glazing and central heating. They reside in these highly controlled environments eating sanitised pre-packaged food from the supermarket and are entertained by multi-channel television. They travel by reliable motor cars to their office, another well controlled environment, where they sit at a desk and consume frequent snacks before returning home in their motor car. The most vigorous exercise during the day is over-forceful tooth brushing. On a Friday night they go out for leventeen pints of sweet, alcoholic lager followed by a bum-burning Vindaloo curry. Not surprisingly, by 45 years of age they have become overweight through too many Calories and not enough exercise. If we then add the effects of cigarette smoking it is easy to see how the all too common 45 year old heart attack victim can occur.

I firmly believe there is a place for alternative forms of therapy and again there are many other doctors who would agree that they can play a role in the holistic care of people. There is a place for herbal remedies, acupuncture, aromatherapy, physiotherapy, osteopaths and chiropractors but, at the same time they have to be kept in their place and within limits. They should all be backed up with recognised science and have a working knowledge of things like Biochemistry, Anatomy and Physiology. Unfortunately, all too often an unqualified and uneducated extreme opinion is given at no little expense with no scientific basis. Doctors and Dentists spend many hard working years learning scientific principles to a high level and then back that up with many further years gaining experience. It is not surprising therefore, that doctors and dentists then find it galling when a patient turns up with some nonsensical quackery. The alternative therapists do themselves no favours when they stray outside of what should be fairly narrow remits and start making outrageous judgements. The value of alternative therapies can perhaps be illustrated in scientific terms by relating them to one area of improved knowledge, which is the role of hormones. There are now literally hundreds of hormones discovered, all of which will control some bodily function which may be large or very small and it is possible that alternative remedies may affect these hormones.

Acupuncture; This ancient practice has potential back up from physiology. It is thought that the acupuncture needles stimulate nerve fibres and thus elicit a response. It is certainly possible that the acupuncture needles could stimulate the basic nervous system together with the Sympathetic side of the Autonomic nervous system. Stimulation of nerves could lead to hormone release and stimulation of the Sympathetic nervous system could lead to many physical effects. It would probably not be possible to stimulate the Para-sympathetic nervous system as it is too deeply buried within the body and therefore Acupuncture may not be able to produce effects to the alimentary tract.

Herbal Remedies; There is an increasing body of evidence that the many chemical substances within these mostly plant based compounds could have effects. Again, the subject of the many minor hormones used by the human body could explain the effects of these compounds.

Aromatherapy; Stimulation of hormone release by these substances is possible.

The above obviously therefore, could offer health benefits to people, but it must be stressed again that outrageous claims must not be made or tolerated. I need to make one thing very clear after 30 years of looking at people's mouths.

It is not possible to diagnose deficiencies
or metabolic disorders simply by
looking at a person's TONGUE.

This stupid idea, which I have come across on a number of occasions recently is the most crass nonsense. Again, there is a complete lack of basic scientific understanding behind these dangerous mis-diagnostic opinions. It is possible to acquire the condition called Glossitis as a sign of iron deficiency anaemia. It is also possible to have glossitis, **in the developing world,** due to deficiencies in Riboflavin (vitamin B2) and Niacin (which is derived from the amino acid tryptophan). You would not see these deficiencies in the developed, western world. Anyone who claims to be able to diagnose these non-existent deficiencies, with no medical testing to confirm it, by simply looking at a person's tongue is showing their uneducated ignorance and is a dangerous charlatan.

An area of life-style advice that I am personally unhappy about is the dieting industry. I fail to understand what is happening with this huge industry and why there is so much nonsense being spouted. I have come to the conclusion that in the background are a group of dominant individuals, who are making a great deal of money whilst hiding the truth from the people they are fleecing. Why else do such large numbers of the population waste their money over potty ideas ? Again, there is no science behind the falsehoods being peddled and absolutely no acknowledgement of the essential subject of Metabolism. It has been known and shown for 40 years that **"dieting makes you fat".** Why doesn't the dieting industry acknowledge this and adjust things accordingly? The more I have learnt and seen as the years have gone by the more it appears that the dieting industry could be accused of being fraudulent. Yet again I see a body of uneducated and unqualified people giving out flawed advice which, far from being beneficial, may in fact be harmful. The incredible thing is we are dealing with a basically simple subject with a basically simple solution, but the dieting industry keeps the answer hidden.

Over the years my frustration at the crass nonsense being peddled grew until I reached a point where I felt the need for further action. My patients were frequently suggesting that I should put my views down on paper and write a book. I rejected this as an unfeasible idea, simply "pie in the sky". I have now written the book. The aim was to write a book about how life worked but, in a form which would be readily understood by the layman, general public who possess no great scientific knowledge. It is not a textbook for use in academic establishments but, at the same time it is a book based strongly on hard scientific facts. I did not wish it to be a book of my personal opinions, although invariably there will be a **small** element of this but, it is a book on irrefutable scientific principles. I make no excuse for the criticism levelled at the unqualified, uneducated, fraudulent quacks, charlatans and gurus who make a living passing on flawed and unsubstantiated advice. There are many of them about, in all walks of life, from the seat of government downwards and if any of them come to read this then I trust it will make them squirm in their embarrassment. Possibly, a mending of the ways could occur and an improved scientific and common sense attitude would prevail.

Having written this book I have subsequently taken advice as to its style and format. With my background it was of no surprise that it was written as a sequential scientific argument. Therefore,

I started off trying to give the basic scientific principles in what I thought were "layman's" terms. It was then made apparent to me that the book was far too technical and I was expecting too much of the layman reader. The book as it stood would be a failure as many potential readers would not get past the first 20 pages. I have therefore decided to revamp the beginning of the book which may result in it becoming confusing but less technical. I personally find the biochemistry of food and its metabolism in the body fascinating and logical but, I of course am somewhat strange and the majority of people would not share my interest. It is still essential that an element of chemistry is introduced at the beginning of the book and I would ask that potential readers try to "stick with it" as I believe the story will be more interesting as you proceed.

Chapter 1
ENERGY

The subject of energy can be a strange and abstract concept. It can be simple to envisage energy in its physical manifestations such as the heat from a fire, light from a light bulb or the phenomenon of electrons passing along a copper wire known as electricity. What about the common kitchen appliance, the refrigerator, where the term energy is perhaps more difficult to comprehend due to the required negative outcome? Energy can also be thought of in terms of work done and this can be graphically illustrated by watching the Olympic games 100metres sprint final when finely conditioned athletes expend large amounts of energy in a very short space of time.

A powerful example of work being done and its relationship to energy is the steam engine. These are of course well known in their role at fairgrounds, on the railways and very importantly as the principal driving force of the industrial revolution. The required work needed is derived from the turning of water to steam by the use of heat and the steam working a piston, which can be used to create movement. A similar effect is produced in the present day by the Internal Combustion Engine where again pistons are moved under the influence of expanding gas to produce the required work or movement. The difference here of course is in the type of fuel used. Whereas in the steam engine it is simply a physical change of water to steam, which is reversible, in the internal combustion engine a fuel is used which is irreversibly changed. When petrol is used in the internal combustion engine the energy obtained to drive the pistons to create the work comes from Chemical energy. Petrol is a mixture of something called Hydrocarbons, containing 7 to 9 carbon atoms, which when mixed with Oxygen (air) and ignited produces an explosion caused by the hydrocarbon molecules breaking up into smaller molecules containing single carbon atoms.

A very important point needs to be made, and it is central to the whole process of energy and life, HYDROCARBONS ACT AS A FUEL. To illustrate this point lets look at something everyone has heard of, Nitroglycerin, the principal ingredient of dynamite. Unfortunately it is necessary to introduce some chemistry but the detail is not important.

$$NO_2 - - - - O - - - - C - - - - C - - - - C - - - - O - - - - NO_2$$

with H above and O, NO_2 below the central C:

```
                      H
                      I
NO2 - - - - O - - - - C - - - - C- - - -C- - - -O- - - -NO2
                      I
                      O
                      I
                     NO2
```

This is the chemical model of nitroglycerin. It has a chain of 3 Carbon atoms. Very often for explosions to occur, Oxygen is required to be present. In the case of nitroglycerin there is already a large amount of Oxygen in the molecule, which is what makes it so unstable and hence useful as an explosive. When nitroglycerin is detonated a huge amount of heat (energy) is released and the reaction can be written thus;

$$4 \ C_3H_5(O.NO_2) - - - - - - \rightarrow 12 \ CO_2 \ + \ 10 \ H_2O \ + \ 6 \ N_2 \ + \ O_2$$

The liquid Nitroglycerin is converted into 4 gaseous products, which have an enormously greater volume. Therefore, the detonation of Nitroglycerin produces a great quantity of heat combined with a great expansion so not surprisingly is a very useful explosive. This great release of energy is due to the violent break-up of the 3-carbon chain.

A very important concept is the process of getting energy from chains of Carbon atoms. Again, it is necessary to introduce some basic organic chemistry. All living organisms are made up mostly of just 4 atoms; Carbon, Oxygen, Hydrogen and Nitrogen. There are lots of other atoms involved but they make a much smaller contribution from a quantity point of view. The 4 major atoms involved in making up the majority of organic molecules join together using something called Covalent Bonds. This is to do with each atom donating an electron to make up the bond. In the case of an atom of Carbon, 4 covalent bonds are made. To make these bonds some energy needs to be applied, and when these bonds are "broken" energy is released /dissipated. This is called the Bond Energy. To illustrate this point lets look at two well known, related molecules, ethyl alcohol and acetylene.

The well-known substance, ethyl alcohol, has two carbon atoms and the chemical formula is written thus;

$$
\begin{array}{ccc}
 & H & H \\
 & I & I \\
C_2H_5OH \quad \text{or} \quad H---C---C---OH \\
 & I & I \\
 & H & H \\
\end{array}
$$

Each - - - line represents a bond, and as can be seen each Carbon atom is associated with 4 bonds. It is a well-known fact that alcohol is a substance high in Calories, which is a measure of the energy contained within the molecule. It is also well known that mixtures with a relatively high alcohol content will burn in air. Consider the lighted Brandy, which was poured over the Christmas pudding. Vaporized mixtures of alcohol in either air or oxygen are explosive, and alcohol has been used as a rocket fuel. The chemical reactions can be represented thus;

$$C_2H_5OH \quad + \quad 3\,O_2 \text{- - - -} \rightarrow \quad 2\,CO_2 \quad + \quad 3\,H_2O$$

Acetylene is related to ethyl alcohol in that it also has 2 Carbon atoms. Like ethyl alcohol it can be burnt in air to give CO_2 and H_2O. However, under the right circumstances, mixed with oxygen, there is violent explosive reaction, which is put to good use. The Oxy-acetylene flame for welding and cutting metal. The difference between ethyl alcohol and acetylene can be easily seen in the chemical formulae.

$$H\text{- - -}C\equiv\!\!\equiv C\text{- - -}H$$

As can be seen, the Carbon atoms still insist on having 4 bonds with the result that the Carbon atoms are joined by a TRIPLE covalent bond. When this Triple bond is broken quickly in one go, then a very large amount of energy is released, allowing the production of an Oxy-acetylene flame.

Although this is a somewhat crude and perhaps inaccurate way of representing Bond Energy, it hopefully will put across the very important concept of how living organisms derive their energy needs. As everyone will appreciate, living organisms do not carry around a furnace with a permanently lit pilot light. They get their energy needs by breaking down, what we know as food and the derivation and storage of that energy occurs by the breaking and making of COVALENT BONDS. This process is known as METABOLISM. It is basically the same in most living organisms, regulated by Hormones and DNA, and controlled by Enzymes. Because the processes involved are so similar, it answers the commonly asked question. Why is there so little difference in the DNA over a wide variety of organisms?

THE CURRENCY OF ENERGY

Human Beings go to work to earn money, in the United Kingdom that means Pounds and Pence, which is then used to service and supply their daily needs. What do living organisms use for "money" which they have earned by assimilating, and using the bond energies of, food products? The answer is a rather complex molecule, which readily "makes and breaks" covalent bonds, and it acts as a receiver, a store, and a donor of energy. This molecule is called ADENOSINE.

Adenosine is made up of two organic molecules joined together and not surprisingly is made up of just 4 types of atom; Carbon, Hydrogen, Oxygen and Nitrogen. The two molecules are something called Adenine, a NUCLEIC ACID, and a RIBOSE sugar. Both of these molecules exhibit a strange habit, which Carbon atoms commonly perform, and that is the formation of circular or RING type structures, instead of the chain type molecules that have already been described. Adenosine is therefore a 3-ringed molecule. An interesting, and as it happens, vital, chemical reaction can now take place between a carbon in the ribose sugar ring and phosphoric acid, resulting in the formation of a new molecule called Adenosine-monophosphate or AMP.

Adenosine-monophoshate can then react with phosphoric acid again and a further phosphate group is attached to the existing phosphate to form Adenosine diphosphate or ADP. Adenosine diphosphate can then react with phosphoric acid and yet another phosphate group is now attached to the developing chain of phosphates and the new molecule Adenosine triphosphate or ATP is formed.

Thus;

Adenosine - - - C- - -*- - -P- - -*- - -P- - -*- - -P

IT IS ATP, WHICH IS THE CURRENCY OF LIFE.

Returning to the subject of bond energies, it is this chain of phosphate groups, which act as the receiver, store and supplier of the energy needs of living organisms. When the bonds marked ★ are made, then energy is received and stored, and when these bonds are broken, then energy is released. Hence, the energy needs of metabolism can be simply thought of in terms of the following reversible reaction, which is taking place continually in all living organisms:

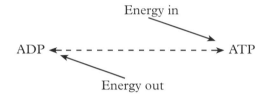

To illustrate this point let's return to the image of the Olympic 100 metres sprint final and the highly conditioned, well muscled athletes taking part. Muscle contraction occurs at the cellular level by one type of muscle fibre, the Actin filaments, sliding over another type called the Myosin filaments. The energy source for this movement to occur comes from the change of ATP to ADP. For further or stronger muscle contractions to occur then more ATP needs to be converted to ADP. The store of ATP in the muscle is obviously limited and therefore it will need to be regenerated. In the short term this occurs by food stores within the muscle being used to convert ADP back into ATP so that further muscle contraction and relaxation can take place, with the result that the sprinter runs. All this is taking place due to the making and breaking of chemical bonds ie. addition or subtraction of a phosphate group. These chemical reactions occur in a time scale different to the one we are generally used to and therefore, at a much faster pace than we can envisage.

What happens when the food supplies within the muscle are used up? More food supplies need to be brought to the muscle via the athlete's blood supply so that the ATP can be regenerated. This of course takes time, although it is what humans would view as a very rapid process. Chemical reactions do take place extremely quickly but, this does go some way to explaining why living organisms, especially 100 metre sprinters, are unable to keep up their very rapid pace for very long. They simply run out of ATP and cannot regenerate it fast enough!

As will be seen later, all living organisms are designed to produce supplies of ATP, and to then use them to carry out all those functions, which constitute life. These include things like movement, nerve function, cell division and cell function at a molecular level. Although, to a degree it sounds as though all living organisms must be awash with ATP, this is not the case as it can be generated very rapidly when needed. But, it does mean that dietary input should only be sufficient to ensure that regeneration of ATP at suitable levels is maintained.

CELL TYPES

Animal Cell

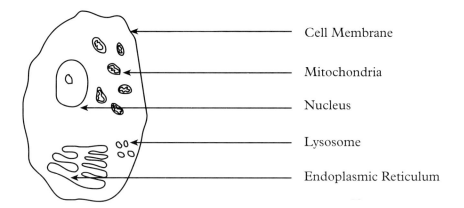

Cell Membrane

Mitochondria

Nucleus

Lysosome

Endoplasmic Reticulum

Plant Cell

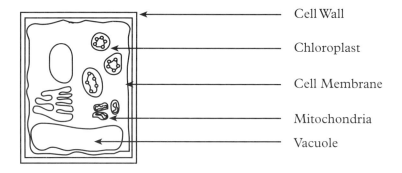

Cell Wall

Chloroplast

Cell Membrane

Mitochondria

Vacuole

The nucleus contains the DNA. The Mitochondria are the "batteries" where ATP is produced.

The Endoplasmic Reticulum is the site of protein production.

Chapter 2
FOOD AND ENERGY PRODUCTION

This chapter will deal with the three major components that are known as FOOD and how these substances are broken down by living organisms so that energy in the form of ATP is produced. Unfortunately, once again a certain amount of chemistry will need to be discussed but every effort will be made to keep this as simple as possible. The fortunate part of this is that once again only the four basic atoms, Carbon, Hydrogen, Oxygen and Nitrogen need be considered.

FAT

The fats and oils used as food are part of a larger group of molecules known as LIPIDS. Lipids have a number of functions for living organisms;

1. Immediate food for energy.
2. Food that is to be stored for later use.
3. Insulation and Protection.
4. In Brain and Nerve tissue, where it plays a vital role in efficient nerve transmission and communication. The brain has a very high Lipid content.
5. A vital constituent of cell membranes.
6. Steroids. Make up some vital hormones and includes the well known molecule, cholesterol.

The Lipids known as fats, which are mostly used for food, are made up of two types of molecule and there can be quite small changes within these molecules to give subtle changes in character. The two molecule types are GLYCEROL which acts as a link or bridge and FATTY ACIDS. Fatty acids are simply long chains of carbon atoms, with hydrogen atoms attached, and specific atom groupings on the ends. There are two groups of Fatty Acids, saturated and unsaturated, and this determines whether the lipid is an oil or a fat. Most people will be aware from media advertisements and advice that the unsaturated fatty acids are supposed to be better for us than the saturated fatty acids. Many people will also be aware that some of the fatty acids are known as essential fatty acids and they have a "code" attached to them such as "omega 3", which are commonly found in fish oils. The code is simply a scientific method of identifying the position of the "double" bonds within the fatty acid chain. A very important fact needs to be made about the role of fats in our diet and its use within our bodies. Flawed elements in the media have given the opinion that fats are simply bad for us and we should not be eating them.

Whilst it is true that the percentage of fat in the diet for many people is too high and should be reduced somewhat, what is not highlighted is that ; OUR BODIES RUN ON FAT BREAKDOWN FOR ENERGY USE ROUTINELY.

People are under the misapprehension that our bodies rely on things like starch and sugar but, in fact we only use these foods for a relatively short time following eating a meal. Most of the time our bodies are using fat for energy needs. The following is an example of the two groups of fatty acids and, when viewing them think in terms of "bond energies" and how many carbon bonds there are to break and release energy. This will give some appreciation of why fats are such "high energy" substances.

Saturated $HOOC-C-C-C-C-C-C-C-C-C-C-C-C-C-CH_3$ FAT

Unsaturated $HOOC-C-C-C-C-C-C==C-C-C-C-C-C-C-CH_3$ OIL

To form what is known as a fat or lipid molecule, 3 fatty acid chains are linked together via the Glycerol molecule to form what is known as a TRIGLYCERIDE. This is what we consume when we eat fat. Glycerol is a molecule with 3 Carbon atoms.

Thus;

```
C - - - Fatty Acid
I
C - - - Fatty Acid
I
C - - - Fatty Acid
```

The Lipids as a whole are water insoluble biological molecules so they therefore repel water. This property is used in the formation of a VERY important structure, called the cell membrane. In place of one of the fatty acid molecules bonding to the glycerol another molecule could bind, and this has a Phosphate group (the phosphate group is similar to that met in AMP, ADP, ATP). The resultant molecule is known as a PHOSPHOLIPID and is integral to cell membranes.

The cell membrane is a double layer of phospholipid, which acts as a highly impervious barrier and hence keeps the cell contents separate from the external environment. The cell membrane has many structures and proteins embedded within it which allows for the controlled passage of substances into and out of the cell. It also acts as the site of many of the chemical reactions of metabolism.

1 typical fatty acid molecule yields over 120 molecules of ATP, for energy use.

PROTEINS

Proteins are required for the following;

1. Food for immediate energy
2. For the production of proteins within living organisms, where they act as essential structures within ALL cells.
3. For the production of ENZYMES and some hormones.

Proteins are made up of chains of relatively small molecules called Amino acids. These chains can be short, containing only between one and two hundred amino acid units or very long, containing many thousands of amino acid units. There are about twenty amino acids, which are used and essential for organic life, and they yet again are composed of the four major atoms Carbon, Hydrogen, Oxygen and Nitrogen. Within two of the amino acids there is found atoms of Sulphur. The amino acids all have basically the same "backbone" within the molecule, and the variation within the amino acids is determined by different "side-chains". Thus;

$$R^\star$$

$$NH_2----C----COOH$$

$$H$$

R⋆ is the "side chain"

To produce the chain which makes up a protein the NH_2 group of one amino acid reacts with the COOH group of another amino acid, with the elimination of H_2O, which leads to the formation of what is known as a "Peptide bond". The Peptide bonds link all the amino acids together producing the long chain molecules called "Proteins".

When members of the animal kingdom eat proteins, they are rapidly broken down into their constituent amino acids and these are then absorbed. The amino acids are then either used for energy production by the breaking of chemical bonds and ATP production OR they are recycled and used to form the necessary proteins required by the living organism. All living cells contain many, many proteins, which are essential for both function and structure.

When the chains of amino acids form, they do not stay in simple straight chains but instead they twist, kink and fold. The reason for this is the size, interaction and influence of the "side chain" parts of the amino acids within the chains. Therefore, proteins can be all sorts of different shapes and the degree of folding can be different for different parts of the chain. To try to demonstrate this let's imagine a simple loop of string, held at two ends and then severely twisted, one end against the other.

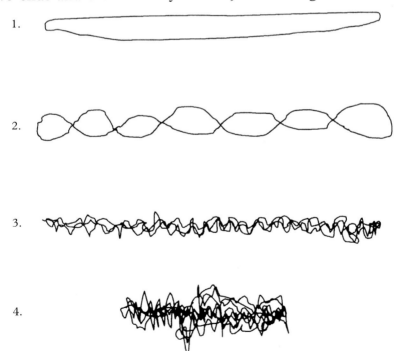

We can end up with a knotted mass, considerably shorter in overall length than the starting point. This is known as the "tertiary " structure of a protein and is very important in both reducing the size/volume of the protein but also is critical for what is a major role of proteins; ENZYMES.

As will be seen later there are very many chemical reactions taking place within cells at a rate which is difficult for humans to envisage. (Over 2000 reactions)These reactions can take place at a rate which may have been accelerated a billion times due to the action of the enzymes. The Enzymes are often present in low concentrations and they are not broken down in the reaction but re-used repeatedly. Without enzymes life would not be possible as we know it and the act of living would be a very, very slow process.

CARBOHYDRATES

Carbohydrates are the most common organic compounds found in nature and the word "Carbohydrate" is an overall term to cover a range of molecules. Carbohydrates are mostly used for energy in animals but in plants there is a significant structural role and it is used in insects to create their external skeleton. Carbohydrates include Monosaccharides, Disaccharides and Polysaccharides and they contain atoms of Carbon, Hydrogen and Oxygen in a ratio of about   1C : 2H : 1O

Monosaccharides;

These are commonly known as the "sugars", which are generally thought of as high-energy food substances. The only monosaccharides that will be dealt with are Glucose, Galactose and Fructose. The chemical formula of these molecules is the same, thus;

$$C_6 H_{12} O_6$$

The number of combinations that this chemical formula could produce, remembering that Carbon atoms seek 4 bonds is considerable, in fact over a dozen variations. It was already seen in the structure of ATP, where the ribose sugar formed a "ring" structure and the same applies to both Glucose and Fructose. Both a ring structure and a chain structure can be envisaged and the minor differences that occur lead to the development of what is known as "isomers".

Disaccharides;
Monosaccharides can link together in pairs to form disaccharides. The common disaccharides are;

Sucrose. This is a pair consisting of Glucose and Fructose molecules.
Lactose. This is a pair consisting of Glucose and Galactose molecules.
Maltose. This is a pair consisting of 2 Glucose molecules.

Polysaccharides;
It is possible to link many units of monosaccharide together and hence form polysaccharides. This process occurs commonly in nature using simply the Glucose monosaccharide and by bonding many thousands of Glucose units, the resulting substance is STARCH. Due to the structure of the Glucose molecule there is much scope for a very "branched" polysaccharide to be produced, and this is exactly what happens with starch. When starch is eaten by living organisms, the digestion process breaks it down into the individual Glucose units. The Glucose is then either used immediately for energy/ATP production or it is stored for future use. In Human beings, that storage material is called GLYCOGEN, which is a many-branched polysaccharide of Glucose units similar to starch. Glucose units can also bond together in a more regular, repeating manner to form long, unbranched chains. This process

is used greatly in the plant kingdom and leads to the formation of CELLULOSE, where 3,000-10,000 units of glucose are used. As is generally known, Cellulose cannot be digested by human beings and it requires special digestion processes, as used by ruminants.

So far it has been somewhat tedious, possibly confusing but unfortunately necessary to describe the foundations of Food science from a chemical point of view. Food has been shown to be basically derived from 4 atoms which are joined together into small molecular units which then link together to form what are known as MACROMOLECULES, which are then broken down by the initial process of digestion back into the small molecular units. The next sections, which may be found more interesting, will describe how those small molecular units are turned into energy.

Having consumed and then digested food it is then broken up into its constituent units before being absorbed by the living organism. These units then follow one of three pathways. They are either used straight away to construct essential molecules which become the building blocks for further organic life. They can be turned into storage compounds for use later and this is another piece of interesting science which should be more openly displayed. It has been made apparent that food products are of 3 basic types and they are all mostly made from just four types of atoms. Nature is wonderful, because whereas scientists would need to go through a very long process in the laboratory, living organisms have the ability to covert the individual molecules making up food from one type to another. This means that if our diet consists say of mostly protein and carbohydrate we would still convert the excess that was not immediately needed into fat to be used later. Our bodies, using a process called "Gluconeogenesis", are readily able to convert fats and proteins into Glucose. As an aside, our brains and kidneys mostly rely on Glucose for energy needs whilst the rest of the body runs happily on fatty acids. So, our constantly maintained glucose blood level is only for the benefit of our brains and kidneys. **If you think about this then it rather makes a mockery of all the silly diets and eating fads.** Our bodies only have a limited capacity for storing Carbohydrate and Protein due to the amount of water that would be naturally associated with these substances but it has an almost unlimited capacity to store fat. Fat is stored as "Adipose tissue" which excludes water.

The third pathway that digested food can take is for it to be immediately broken down and turned into energy. The first food product used following a meal is the carbohydrate element which is readily broken down into its monosaccharides and this can be represented by this following chemical reaction.

$$C_6 H_{12} O_6 + 6O_2 \xrightarrow{\text{Enzymes}} 6CO_2 + 6H_2O + \text{Energy}$$

Glugose   Oxygen   Carbon Dioxide   Water

As can be seen, there are two vitally important parts to this reaction; one is the need for oxygen and the other is the need for Enzymes. The breakdown of Glucose takes place using three processes and if these processes were to be mimicked by scientists in the laboratory it would take rather a long time. In nature, these processes take place much more quickly because they are controlled by a series of enzymes which can act like a production line in a factory passing the product of each reaction further down the conveyor belt.

GLYCOLYSIS

The first process is called glycolysis and takes place without the need for Oxygen. It requires an input of ATP to in effect "prime" the Glucose, early in the process but there is a net yield at the end of it. The full chemical process will not be described here, but there are 10 steps and each of them requires control by an enzyme. The end result is that one molecule of 6 Carbon atoms Glucose is converted to two molecules of 3 Carbon atoms Pyruvate. The Glycerol part of Triglycerides can be directed into this pathway and some amino acids can be converted to Pyruvate, so you can see that fat and protein molecules can also be utilized. Initially, ATP has to be used but ATP is generated during glycolysis to give a net gain of two ATP molecules. The Pyruvate produced has two possible fates. When Oxygen is present, it is broken down further into carbon dioxide and water plus more energy and in the absence of Oxygen it is turned into Lactic Acid.

Let us now return to the 100 metres Olympic final. The athletes have trained hard and have got their bodies and necessary muscles into peak condition. They are about to work those muscles for about 10 seconds and during that time they may well not actually breathe! They require ATP to make their muscles work. Within the muscles they have a limited supply of already made ATP and a store of some Glucose. During the race they will have difficulty in getting sufficient Oxygen into the muscles to deal with the Pyruvate, which will be produced during the breakdown of the stores of Glucose. The Pyruvate under these conditions will be converted to Lactic Acid and the muscles will run out of Energy. Hence, the sprinters will not be able to sustain their speed for very much more than the distance they have run.

The Pyruvate, which is produced by the process of Glycolysis then comes under the influence of yet another Enzyme, which converts it into a molecule containing two atoms of Carbon and a molecule of carbon dioxide, is released. The molecule containing the two Carbon atoms is called an ACETYL molecule.

$$Pyruvate - - - - - - - \rightarrow Acetyl\ +\ CO_2$$
$$Enzyme$$

An important point now needs to be made. When Fats, Proteins and other Carbohydrates are broken down into their constituent units by their own Enzyme driven pathways, the final point reached is this same two Carbon acetyl molecule. So, all the other food products which have been consumed and digested and which are to be used for energy production, come to this final point.

The Acetyl molecule then combines with an acceptor molecule called COENZYME A (CoA) to form Acetyl CoA and this enters a breakdown pathway, which is normally viewed as a cycle. This takes place in the centre of an intracellular body called a MITOCHONDRIA, which were previously pointed out as the BATTERIES of LIFE. This cycle is known under a number of names; The Tricarboxylic Acid (TCA) cycle, The Citric Acid cycle or The Krebs cycle. Once the Acetyl CoA has entered the cycle the CoEnzyme A is released to link up with another Acetyl molecule.

KREBS CYCLE

Two Carbon Acetyl molecules join with a four Carbon molecule to form a six Carbon molecule. This six Carbon molecule is then broken down by a series of Enzymes and the original two Carbon molecules are released as carbon dioxide.

The original four Carbon molecule is reformed and hence the whole sequence can start again. NOW, those of you who have not been thoroughly confused by all of this may be asking yourself "so where is the energy?"

So far it has been shown how a six Carbon atom, molecule of Glucose has been broken down into six molecules of CO_2 and this means three molecules of Oxygen (O_2) must have been used. Thus;

$$C_6 \ O_6 \ (H_{12}) \ + \ 3O_2 \ \dashrightarrow \ 6CO_2 \ + \ (H_{12})$$

    Glugose   Oxygen   Carbon Dioxide

As you can see something is not accounted for. There are twelve atoms of Hydrogen, which are left over. It is these twelve Hydrogen atoms, which are important in the production of ATP. Although it has not been shown during the process of Glycolysis and during a turn of the Krebs cycle, at various points the Hydrogen atoms have been taken up by special molecules called Hydrogen Acceptors. These Hydrogen acceptor molecules carry the Hydrogen atoms and then release them when needed into a complicated process called the ELECTRON TRANSPORT CHAIN.

The Mitochondria contained within cells can be thought of as a double skinned body. The Krebs cycle takes place inside the inner skin of the Mitochondria and the Electron Transport Chain is contained within the inner skin or better known as the inner membrane. The Mitochondria inner membrane is a convoluted structure, which gives it a large surface area, and it divides the Mitochondria into two compartments.

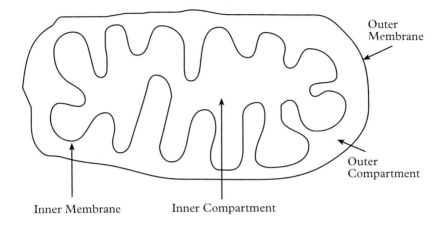

Outer
Membrane

Outer
Compartment

Inner Membrane   Inner Compartment

ELECTRON TRANSPORT CHAIN

The electron transport chain is a very complicated process and scientists have still not got the complete picture of how it works and what exactly happens. Much of the early work was "educated guesses" and it has been a question of trying to match observed results with theory. One has to remember that Mitochondria are extremely small bodies (organelles) that were only discovered with the development of the electron microscope in the last 50 years or so. Their purpose in life then only became apparent with the development of very high-speed centrifuges, which allowed for the separation of the intra-cellular organelles into layers in a test tube depending upon their density. It could then be established that Mitochondria took up oxygen and produced ATP. It is not important to go into details of the Electron Transport Chain. Those people who are interested will easily find the relevant information.

Hydrogen atoms are often thought of, from a chemical point of view, as a combination of a Hydrogen ion, H+ (a proton), and an electron (e¨). Thus

$$H - - - - - - - - - \blacktriangleright \ H+ \ \ + \ \ E-$$
$$\text{Proton} \qquad \text{Electron}$$

When the Hydrogen atoms, which are produced from the breakdown of Glucose, are carried by their acceptor molecules into the Electron Transport Chain, the atoms are split into a proton and an electron. The electron is passed through a series of molecules known as Cytochromes whilst the protons are pumped into the outer compartment of the Mitochondria. The result is the outer compartment has both a concentration of Hydrogen ions as well as a concentration of "positive charge", known as a Chemiosmotic effect. The charged, concentrated Hydrogen ions then move through a special channel in the inner mitochondrial membrane from the outer compartment into the inner compartment, where they react with both the electron that has passed down the electron transport chain and Oxygen to form water (H_2O). On passing through the special channel in the inner membrane the critical event takes place and

ADP is converted into ATP

For each passage of a Hydrogen ion through the special channel, 3 molecules of ATP are produced. There are two points that now need to be made;

For every molecule of Glucose that is broken down into CO_2 and H_2O then potentially about three dozen molecules of ATP are produced.

ATP production can be disconnected from the special channel and the energy from the passing Hydrogen ions is released as HEAT. This is known as THERMOGENESIS.

1 molecule of glucose yields about 36 molecules of ATP.

Compare this with the yield from a typical fatty acid of over 120 ATP molecules, and then remember that a typical fat molecule is 3 chains of fatty acids joined together by a 3 carbon glycerol molecule. The ATP yield from a typical fat molecule is therefore over 10 times the yield from a glucose molecule.

BASAL METABOLIC RATE

As has been demonstrated, the process of food product breakdown is made efficient and possible by very clever molecules called Enzymes. Living organisms rely on Enzymes to carry out a huge number of chemical reactions, which make up that thing known as life. This process is known as Metabolism and it is divided into two parts depending upon whether something is being taken apart, CATABOLISM, or something is being constructed, ANABOLISM. A fascinating aspect of these processes is that for many of the chemical reactions taking place, the same Enzyme is used. Living organisms spend a vast amount of their time carrying out the process of Anabolism, which we would call growth and repair. In the plant world, the majority of their time and energy is spent on growth. This leads to things like the production of wood from trees and the weekly Sunday morning ritual of mowing the lawn. In the animal kingdom growth tends to slow down and stop (apart from girth perhaps) and most Anabolic processes are related to the repair of damaged, and the replacement of expended, tissues. This is seen in things such as the continuous loss of skin cells, which leads to the common domestic phenomenon known as dust. All of this growth, repair and replacement use the food, which is either produced or taken in, depending upon the organism concerned, whose breakdown products are the building blocks for new tissues. THIS PROCESS REQUIRES A SOURCE OF ENERGY. Thus, anabolism requires some catabolism to take place first. Also, living organisms within the animal kingdom frequently have a need to in effect have their own internal central heating systems and they must retain a constant internal temperature (Enzymes only tend to work at a very narrow range of temperatures). They therefore have to have a means of producing heat and THIS PROCESS REQUIRES A SOURCE OF ENERGY.

A common misconception is that living organisms use the majority of their energy supplies to carry out movement. This is NOT the case. The majority of energy intake and NEEDS are to carry out anabolic processes and to keep warm. This, in effect minimal energy need, is known as the BASAL METABOLIC RATE. This is a very, very, very important concept, which will be returned to later. This means that there are a daily number of calories, which need to be available even if no work is done. CINDERELLA still had a basal metabolic rate whilst awaiting her Prince Charming. The GREATEST problem facing the present modern world is ensuring that all humans on the planet have sufficient energy (food) intake to answer the daily basal metabolic rates and so avoid starvation.

The immediate question that everyone will now be asking himself or herself maybe, is what is my basal metabolic rate? The second question may well be, can I alter my basal metabolic rate? The answer to both questions of course will depend upon circumstances.

Those people with a highly active life carrying out heavy manual work or playing a great deal of physical sport will tend to have a higher basal metabolic rate whilst at the same time requiring more calorie intake to answer their physical needs. Having developed a higher basal metabolic rate they may well retain it. On the other hand those people with a more sedentary life and those people already alluded to in poorer environments that are not getting sufficient food will have a lower basal metabolic rate. Hence their calorie intake needs will be depressed. When human beings go on a diet, with no change in lifestyle, then they lower their basal metabolic rate and it may stay depressed. Again, this is something, which will be returned to later.

Basal metabolic rate is higher in taller and heavier people. It tends to decrease as we get older and has a genetic component which means it varies from person to person. As a general rule the following shows how important Basal Metabolic rate is as these are the percentages of daily energy use.

Basal Metabolic Rate	60 - 70%
Heat Production (Thermogenesis)	10%
Exercise and movement	20 - 30%

Chapter 3
PHOTOSYNTHESIS

Due to the thought processes of scientists in the past it became accepted that the animal kingdom was somehow superior to other forms of life. It was quite common in textbooks dealing with evolutionary subjects to come across ideas, which placed animals above plants. This is not altogether surprising because after all the animal kingdom is populated by species, which possess brains as well as the ability to move around. Before the development of the microscope, plants must have appeared to be pretty primitive organisms with little internal structure compared to animals, which of course had highly developed internal arrangements. In earlier texts therefore we could come across things like a pyramid of life with mankind at the summit. Thus;

Man

Monkeys/Apes

Carnivorous Animals

Herbivorous   Animals

Amphibians   and   Reptiles

Fish, Whales and other Water Creatures

Trees, Shrubs and other Flowering Plants

Grasses, Mosses, Fungi, Seaweeds and Ferns

In their ignorance life could also be represented as a stairway thus;

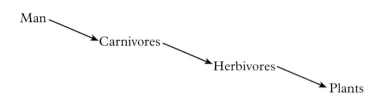

So, mankind was superior together with the rest of the animal kingdom. OH, REALLY. It does not take much thought to realize that without grass for the ruminants and cattle to graze on, there would be no Herbivores for Carnivores to feed off. Therefore, without Plant life there could be NO life, as we presently know it!!!!! But of course, this still did not alter the fact that Plant life must be a very low form of life. After all, who ever thought of a tree getting up and moving around? OH, REALLY AGAIN. Let us examine the lifestyle of the animal kingdom for a moment. As everyone knows, and as has already been shown, to derive their energy so that life can take place, ANIMALS HAVE TO EAT FOOD. They are HETEROTROPHIC. Now let us consider the Plant kingdom. Plants derive their energy requirements in a completely different manner. They use Light, principally Sunlight to produce their OWN food. They do not need to eat. They are AUTOTROPHIC.

All of a sudden plants do not seem quite so low and stupid. Indeed, even the humble grass plant is in fact a highly complex organism with many of the metabolic pathways present which are present in so called higher organisms, such as Mankind. In fact the only way that the humble grass plant is inferior to species of the animal kingdom is its lack of mobility and lack of a brain!!!!!!! Plants otherwise have many similarities in that they interact with the atmosphere, have an internal system of fluid movement, have a series of Hormones for control purposes, use similar molecules for both Anabolism and Catabolism, indulge in sexual practices, produce waste products and rely heavily on water for life.

Plants take in through their root system Water and all of the essential nutrients required for the production of all of the necessary molecules needed for life. They therefore take in Nitrogen, Phosphorus, Potassium, Calcium, Magnesium, Sulphur, Iron, Sodium, Chlorine, Copper, Manganese, Cobalt, Zinc, Boron and Molybdenum. Plants then take in through the pores in their leaves, called Stomata, carbon dioxide from the atmosphere, which means they have a supply of Carbon, Oxygen and Hydrogen, and therefore have all the atoms needed for the production of the molecules of life.

The quite wonderful phenomena can then take place, which is the conversion of Carbon dioxide taken in from the atmosphere combined with Water taken in by the roots to form GLUCOSE and release Oxygen. Thus;

$$6CO_2 \quad + \quad 6H_2O \quad - - - - - \blacktriangleright \quad C_6\,H_{12}\,O_6 \quad + \quad 6O_2$$

| Carbon Dioxide | Water | Glugose | Oxygen |

From this starting point all further Carbohydrates, Fats and Proteins, together with other essential molecules can be produced.

It cannot be emphasized enough how important this process is. Without it there would be no higher life-forms on the planet but simply single celled primitive organisms who could live without Oxygen. If we were to go back in time many millions of years we would come across a planet with an atmosphere largely made up of carbon monoxide and carbon dioxide and perhaps methane. Living organisms consisted of single celled bacteria, which survived, in the surface of the oceans using Hydrogen Sulphide in their metabolic processes. With evolution there developed a simple organism, which started to release Oxygen molecules into the atmosphere. This process developed until a state of mutual benefit, called symbiosis, occurred between these early organisms and a new organism was born which was more efficient, with a superior metabolism using the Oxygen being produced. This organism captured the light energy from the Sun and used it to create more advanced molecules from the readily available carbon dioxide and water. Over millions of years these early organisms gradually changed the hostile atmosphere so that more Oxygen was present. These early Oxygen producing organisms are the forerunners of our modern day plants and their offspring are still seen today populating the surface waters of our oceans. They are called Blue-Green Bacteria and are present in vast quantities in seawater and they form the starting point of aquatic food chains. From these simple organisms more complex aquatic organisms developed among which were those known as Algae which range from small simple organisms to larger organisms know commonly as Sea-weeds. It is thought that it was these organisms, which moved onto land, by perhaps becoming specialized at living on the seashore, and hence developing into plants.

The vitally important point that must be stressed is that the process of Photosynthesis produces as a waste product a great deal of Oxygen whilst taking in and profitably using carbon dioxide gas which is damaging to the atmosphere of our planet. It is no surprise therefore, and in fact very sensible, if some members of the human race create a fuss about things like de-forestation and pollution of our oceans. It is the production of Oxygen by the plant kingdom, and that includes the blue-green bacteria in the ocean, which allows the rest of the living organisms to LIVE. At the present time we are all designed to use atmospheric Oxygen at its current proportion within the atmosphere we are currently living in, so we depend on the level of plant life currently existing.

Photosynthesis takes place in plant tissue, which is green in colour, which means it is mostly in those parts known as leaves. Within the plant cells there are organelles called chloroplasts and it is in these that the light gathering activity takes place to provide the energy for the Anabolic process of turning carbon dioxide and water into Glucose. The chloroplasts are full of a molecule called CHLOROPHYLL. Chlorophyll is a "tadpole shaped" molecule, which if you haven't already guessed is made up of Carbon, Hydrogen, Oxygen and Nitrogen with 55 atoms of Carbon. Sitting in the middle of the "head" of the molecule is one atom of MAGNESIUM. Those readers who are gardeners will be aware that plants can easily suffer from a type of Chlorosis due to Magnesium deficiency, which is cured by a spray of Epsom salts, and which manifests as a lack of green colouration.

THE PROCESS

It is not the intention or purpose of this book to go into great details about the actual workings of photosynthesis. The process of photosynthesis is a series of very complicated chemical reactions combined with a number of complex processes, the workings of which are still not known in absolute detail. There are many other books on this subject that can be read if more detail is required.

There are a number of slightly different Chlorophyll molecules and they are highly organized within the Chloroplasts of plant cells. Depending upon which type of Chlorophyll molecule is looked at then the light absorbing properties will vary. The light used is in what is known as the visible spectrum, which has a range of between 390 and 780 nanometers. Chlorophyll mostly uses Violet-Blue light of about 450 nanometers and Red light of about 670 nanometers. The Chlorophyll molecules are grouped together and act like an Antenna, focusing their light harvesting onto one spot to increase efficiency, known as a PHOTOSYSTEM. The light energy absorbed is converted into chemical energy resulting in the following events.

1. Water molecules (H_2O) are split apart. It is necessary for this to take place in the presence of the element Manganese. The manganese is not actually "used" but simply acts, as a form of catalyst, so very little is needed. The result of this is Oxygen gas is released which is passed into the atmosphere. Thus

$$2H_2O \ + \ \text{Light Energy} \ \text{- - - -} \longrightarrow \ O_2 \ + \ 4H+ \ + \ e\text{-}$$

	Mn	Proton Electron

As can be seen there are similarities to the Electron Transport Chain and ATP production.

2. A concentration of H+ (protons) build up leading to a situation where ATP is produced from ADP ie Energy. The electrons produced are sent along a pathway, being passed from one molecule to another.

3. The electrons and protons are then taken up by a carrier molecule, similar to those used in Glucose catabolism, and the resultant Hydrogen atoms are fed into the cycle, which turns Carbon dioxide into Glucose.

Having harvested the light energy and turned it into both ATP and a molecule carrying Hydrogen atoms, plants then carry out a series of Enzyme controlled reactions which turns CO_2 into glucose and water. There are a number of different pathways, which can be taken, but the most common is called The CALVIN CYCLE. Basically, under the control of an Enzyme called RUBISCO which is the worlds MOST abundant protein, the carbon dioxide is combined with a 5 Carbon sugar molecule, to form a 6 Carbon molecule which immediately splits into two 3 Carbon molecules. With the use of the energy stored in the ATP, the Hydrogen atoms are then incorporated into these 3 Carbon molecules and the overall result is one molecule of Glucose and the regeneration of the original 5 Carbon sugar molecule.

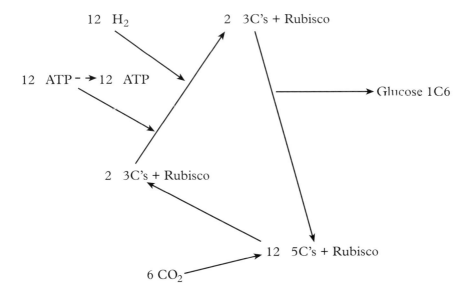

From this Glucose molecule the plant can then either use it for energy use (growth), storage (starch) or the production of Proteins and Fats.

ALL FROM SUNLIGHT!

FACTS ABOUT PHOTOSYNTHESIS

The estimated sugar production, EACH YEAR, from green organisms is 100 - 200 BILLION metric tons.

40 - 50% of the Oxygen in the atmosphere comes from oceans and lakes. This is produced by BLUE-GREEN bacteria and ALGAE, which are very susceptible to Pollutants from agriculture and industry. Things like DDT are extremely harmful to these aquatic green organisms and if they are not looked after then there will be NO oxygen released back into the atmosphere.

One acre of Corn, (10,000 plants), accumulates over 5,000 pounds of Carbon in a growing season. This requires an intake of 10 metric tons of CO_2. The proportion of CO_2 in the atmosphere is 0.039%. This means that atmospheric is continually being removed and replaced so that it remains constant.

The Oxygen that is released by green organisms comes from the water (H_2O) that is taken in and not from the CO_2 taken in. Therefore the full Photosynthetic reaction is more accurately written as;

$$6CO_2 \; + \; \text{Light Energy} \; - - \rightarrow \; C_6H_{12}O_6 \; + \; 6O_2 \; + \; 6H_2O$$

Most of the water taken in by plants is used for the process called Transpiration, (which is the passage of water taken in by the roots, passed through the plant, and expired through the leaves) with less than 1% used in photosynthesis.

The wavelength of light, which reaches the Earth, is determined by the filtering action of the upper atmosphere. This is commonly called the OZONE LAYER. As has already been stated the process of photosynthesis takes place using clearly defined wavelengths of light. Therefore, if due to changes in the upper atmosphere (caused by irresponsible actions of Human beings) the wavelength of light is appreciably altered then the consequences for green organisms could be serious. This of course would have consequences for ALL living organisms and is one of the reasons that scientists view atmospheric changes so seriously.

Chapter 4
GENETICS

The subject of Genetics tends to immediately make many members of the population "bring the shutters down" and refuse to try to comprehend the subject. This no doubt is caused by what used to be the standard teaching of this subject in schools. The subject of Genetics at one time was based on the work of the Moravian monk called Gregor Mendel and his work on Peas. One of Gregor Mendel's strong points was mathematics and his important work was heavily based on mathematics. Unfortunately, when the subject of Genetics was taught to students the emphasis was the mathematical theories / findings that were produced by Mr Mendel. The end result for many people was something of a turn-off. Most people perhaps will remember that there were terms such as dominant and recessive and that there was something called a ratio of three to one. Whilst these concepts are still vitally useful today for "plant breeders" and researchers into genetic diseases, the new knowledge gained into DNA makes the subject of Genetics a much more fascinating topic and there is not quite so much need for obscure mathematics. As will hopefully be shown in the rest of this chapter Nature has been absolutely incredible in inventing what is essentially a very simple concept which has allowed life to evolve and produce the vital system called inheritance.

The picture called the Fluid Mosaic which is to be found in many modern text books on any subject with a biological content is quite wonderful and represents the very essence of Life itself. Cell membranes were, until relatively recently, thought of as simple barriers which kept the cell contents within the cell and the external environment outside. The whole idea of a cell being a "balloon filled with water" is now thought to be wrong and membranes are now viewed as very important structures. Cell membranes are now thought of as dynamic, functional structures, which perhaps would best be thought of as the surface of the Sea, always in motion and always changing. This concept is shown in textbooks as a fluid mosaic but there is much, much more to membranes than this. Going back to earlier chapters, rudimentary catabolism was described with the breakdown of Glucose into its constituent parts and the production of energy. This process was controlled by a large number of enzymes, which are in fact Proteins. The breakdown of Glucose occurs, in our measure of time, very quickly. From a practical point of view, try to imagine all of the steps, which are taken in the breakdown of Glucose and all of the Enzymes, which are needed, and then envisage that process in a "balloon filled with water". Obviously, this process cannot take place under the conditions described, as it is too inefficient and leaves too much to chance. The whole thing has got to be far more organized. Step up to the podium, MEMBRANES.

The Fluid Mosaic picture is shown with lots of strange shapes embedded in it. These strange shapes are representative of the large range of Proteins, which have a role in the workings of the cell. Some of them act as transporters, passing different molecules in and out of the cell. Some act as aerials, collecting messages from outside and passing them inside the cell. Some act as Enzymes for the different metabolic processes and, they do not act in isolation. Imagine now, a conveyor system attached to the membrane, which takes in a Glucose molecule at one end and then passes it from one Enzyme to the next, while it is slowly taken to pieces. Only it is not slow but extremely rapid and very, very organized. In this case the membrane is probably the outer membrane of the Mitochondria so that the final products of this catabolism can quickly be transferred into the required breakdown/energy production chain. WHERE DO THESE ENZYMES AND PROTEINS COME FROM? The answer is the Cell produces them and it does so because of Genetics. The Fluid Mosaic far from representing a moving barrier represents the very essence of LIFE itself, as it represents Energy production linked to the workings of DNA.

Many people will be aware that in different parts of the world in recent times there has been an obscure event-taking place, which has caused what appears to be unwarranted excitement. The Human Genome Project. To most people this would look like a badly put together telephone directory in a completely alien language. The Human Genome Project represents a "map" of the sequence of the DNA of Human beings. BUT WHAT IS THIS "MAGICAL" SUBSTANCE CALLED DNA? It is really quite simple.

"DNA is a code for the production of Proteins" That is all it does. LIFE is determined by the enzymic affect of Proteins. Genetics has become the study of a simple code for the joining together of Amino Acids to form Proteins. THAT IS ALL DNA DOES!!

If we now return to the picture of the Fluid Mosaic, it now becomes obvious why it represents so much more than a simple barrier. It is a graphic illustration of the end product of DNA with all the Enzymes embedded in the membrane which control Metabolism, and hence Life. All living organisms are reliant on DNA, and all living organisms are simply functioning because of the controlling influence of Proteins acting as Enzymes. Far from being a complicated system with a lot of complicated mathematics, it turns out that Genetics "in principle" is a relatively simple process because all it is, is a simple code for the production of Proteins. It really needs to be repeated; ALL DNA DOES IS CODE FOR THE PRODUCTION OF PROTEINS.

THE STRUCTURE OF DNA

The previous few paragraphs have continually hinted that DNA is just a simple code, which is most certainly what it is. DNA is made up essentially of just FOUR molecules. These four molecules are of two types, one type is called a Purine and the other type is called a Pyrimidine. The Purines are called Adenine and Guanine, and the Pyrimidines are called Cytosine and Thymine. We have already come across Adenine, it is the foundation of the molecules of energy, ATP. All of these molecules are "ring" structures made up of Carbon, Hydrogen, Oxygen and Nitrogen, just like other molecules in earlier chapters. These four molecules, which are called the "Bases", combine with a molecule of a Ribose sugar and a phosphate group to form what is known as a "Nucleotide". Thus;

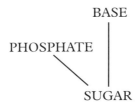

Depending upon the structure of the Ribose Sugar gives either DNA or RNA.

RNA   Ribonucleic Acid
DNA   DeOxy-Ribonucleic Acid

The individual Nucleotides link together via a Sugar - - -> Phosphate link to form chains which creates what is known as DNA molecules and these chains obviously have a long series of "Base molecules" running along the edge of them. The Four "Base molecules" are known by their initial letter so we have;

A   =   adenine
G   =   guanine
C   =   cytosine
T   =   thymine

The chain created could thus look something like;

A G C T T T G C C A A G C T A A A C C G T T T G G C A G T C A G T C G T A G

Ie. The order is apparently totally random.

We now come to the clever bit, which led to great excitement in the late 1950's, and resultant Nobel prizes. It turns out that the "Bases" naturally pair off with each other so that Adenine always tries to link to Thymine and Guanine always tries to link with Cytosine. The result is two chains running parallel with each other with weak bonds binding the two chains together.

A G C T T T G C A A G C T A A A C C G T T T G G C A G T C A G T C G T A G

T C G A A A C G T T C G A T T T G G C A A A C C G T C A G T C A G C A T C

Because of the molecular configuration these two chains twist around each other to form the famous "HELIX" which has become the symbol for both DNA and Genetics. This "Helix" then twists and wraps itself into a bigger, broader structure, which eventually becomes what is known as a "CHROMOSOME". The Chromosomes contain many hundreds of millions of "Bases". But, what is the point of all of these paired Bases. This work is being written on a computer, which functions by using a Digital code which younger members of the population will have some grasp of. The chain of "Bases" is also simply a digital code based on the four digits A, G, C, T.

If you were to take any Three of these Four digits how many combinations are there? The answer is 64.

For example, starting with "A" we could have;

AAA, AAG, AAC, AAT, AGG, ACC,
ATT, AGC, AGA, AGT, etc.

There are twenty "Amino Acids" which make up Proteins. So if we allot say three of these combinations to each amino acid, and also have combinations for Start, Pause and Stop then you can see that 64 combinations is about right. Each of these combinations is called a "CODON" and therefore DNA is simply a code of 64 Codons .It can now be readily seen that DNA acts as a chain of instructions for a series of Amino Acids which when joined together produce a Protein. Simple! That is all there is to molecular Genetics and the whole thing is so beautifully done it most certainly should not be a "turn-off" for anybody.

There are of course still many processes still to go through and the very complicated details are still being investigated and worked out. So how is a protein made? The DNA is stored in the Nucleus of the cell and the reason for two complementary chains is about to be explained. The Chromosome can be thought of as a "Zipper". When a protein needs to be made, the part of the chromosome containing the code for it is "Unzippped". By natural pairing off of the four bases a copy of the coded piece of chromosome can be produced and this can act as a "template" for the correct sequence of Amino Acid units to build up a Protein.

```
A C G T A C G T A C G T          A C G T A C G T A C G T
T G C A T G C A T G C A      A       T
                               C     G
                                 G   C
                                  T    A
                                  A    T
                                   C    G
                                     G   C
                                      T    A
                                      A    T
                                       C    G
                                         G   C
                                          T    A
```

As can be seen, in the first diagram is a short chain of DNA with paired off bases. In the second diagram the paired off bases have "unzipped" and this allows a new sequence of bases to be formed, which naturally has the same sequence as the original. The DNA chain has to "unzip" because the DNA chain is heavily folded and twisted within the chromosome. As can be seen though, there is now a copy of one half of the DNA chain, which is separate and can now be used for the production of a Protein. This section of the DNA chain is known as a GENE.

Let us imagine that having unfolded and "unzipped" the DNA chain has produced a sequence of bases, 1000 bases long. Remember that three bases make up a codon, and allowing for starting, pausing and finishing, this means we have the Template for a Protein of about 300 Amino Acids. It should be pointed out that this sequence of bases is connected to a slightly different sugar molecule and this whole structure is known as RNA. It also needs pointing out that the THYMINE base in the RNA structure is replaced by a very similar molecule called URACIL and so strictly speaking the sequence of bases should have the letter "U" and not "T". This RNA structure, which is the Template for Protein, is known as   MESSENGER RNA. The MESSENGER RNA is formed in the Nucleus of the cell, which are where the chromosomes are stored, and its next task is to leave to find the site within the cell of Protein production.

The Messenger RNA moves to a part of the cell called the RIBOSOME, which is perhaps best thought of as a form of Knitting Machine. Within the cell cytoplasm are a number of molecules called TRANSFER RNA which can perhaps be envisaged as "hook like" in appearance. On one end of the TRANSFER RNA is a "codon" of three bases which pair off with the "codon" in the MESSENGER RNA and on the opposite end of the TRANSFER RNA is attached the appropriate Amino Acid. As the MESSENGER RNA is fed into the RIBOSOME the appropriate TRANSFER RNA is attached at the "codons". The result is a series of Amino Acids are brought together and Peptide bonds are formed. The end result is a Protein is formed.

FACTS ABOUT DNA

In the recent past there has been a lot of media coverage of something called "The Human Genome" project. This has basically been research and laboratory investigations into the sequence of bases which make up our chromosomes and the results when published would not look very interesting as it will simply be lots of A, C, G & T's. The following dramatically demonstrates the glory of Nature and the brilliance of the essentially simple code that is DNA.

There are 3,000,000,000 letters in the human DNA alphabet.

Each cell has about 6 feet of DNA. (just under 2 metres)

If you imagine the whole Genome laid out in a straight line from Lands End to John O'Groats via London (New York to Chicago) then it would be about 1000 miles. There would be 50 bases for every inch and about 3,000,000 bases for every mile.

There are about 50,000 - - - - - 100,000 Genes in the human Genome producing about 50,000 - - - - - 100,000 proteins.

Genes range from about 500 to over 2,000,000 bases and the Genes can be arranged in related families within the chromosomes.

A lot of the Genome appears to be what is described as "Junk". This means most of the Genome does not act as Genes but is often simply a large number of endless repeats of bases apparently doing nothing.

Two people may differ in about one DNA base letter in every thousand. This means about 3 million changes.

Over 98% of our Genome is similar to that of Chimps, Mice and Rabbits. This is not really surprising as our metabolic pathways are virtually the same so the Proteins/Enzymes required are the same.

An interesting side shoot of the Genome is a cell organelle already discussed previously, The Mitochondria. Mitochondria have their own section of DNA separate to that in the chromosomes contained in the nucleus. This piece of DNA has about 16,000 bases. Mitochondria are passed on, inheritance wise, from mothers. There are generally no mitochondria found within Sperm but they are found in the Eggs that sperm are to fertilize. This has been put to use by Scientists when studying Evolution as the DNA in mitochondria provide a link to previous generations and can be a method of determining relationships between different races of people.

An event can occur in a number of ways which can cause serious consequences; MUTATION. Changes can occur to the base sequence of the DNA .If this change occurs to a sequence containing a Gene then this could lead to a change in "codon" and therefore a change in Amino Acid. This might possibly lead to severe changes in the Protein so that any Enzymic action is altered with obviously potential problems with metabolism. This can be demonstrated in the disorder called Cystic Fibrosis where there is a change to a protein, which spans a cell membrane and alters the Sodium levels in the cell.

Mutation can occur due to Chemical, Radioactive or Environmental Pollutants causing changes to the DNA base sequence. If this change were to occur in the Germ cells (sperm or eggs) then there is the possibility of causing a genetic disease in offspring. If this change was to occur in other tissues then cell division may be altered and Cancer could be the end result. Over a long period of time then subtle changes brought about by mutation, which may not be harmful, could lead to the process known as Evolution.

One further point about changes to DNA, Aging. At the end of chromosomes are areas of DNA bases called TELOMERES. With each cell division these Telomeres get a little shorter. In babies telomeres are about 20,000 bases long but in a 60 year old they may be less than 10,000 bases long. Telomeres act as a control over cell death and the shorter the telomere the more likely cell death will occur. In Cancer this control seems to be turned off so that cell division takes place abnormally.

Another area, which has appeared in recent times, is CLONING. This process is the development of a new organism without going through sexual reproduction and the union of two "half sets" of chromosomes. What happens is that the full set of chromosomes is taken from a cell (not the cells of Sex), and a new organism is grown from this starting point. Because the DNA used has not been altered it means the Cloned organism is an exact replica of the original organism. One very big problem is that the Telomeres are not the Telomeres of a young cell but of an older cell. This has the effect of producing a young organism (the Clone) with old DNA and so making the organism susceptible to the diseases of old age, at a young age.

GENETIC MODIFICATION

As has been seen, a Gene is a sequence of bases, and scientists have been able to take these Genes from one organism and splice them into the GENOME of another organism. Scientists have argued that this is simply an acceleration of the normal process of Nature, but this is being somewhat economical with the truth and is probably nothing more than an attempt at justifying a commercial act with a great deal of money at stake.

Mankind has over the centuries used the process of Genetic Mutation and Selective Breeding to produce the plants and animals that we care for and rely on. This is a number of processes, which Charles Darwin wrote about in the 1800's, and perhaps can be best called Survival of the Fittest. Through the process of Genetic Mutation, occasionally a "superior" example of a species may occur which Mankind may have deliberately cultivated for his own use. This of course is also part of the natural process of evolution. Mankind has then taken this process further by selectively breeding two members of the **SAME SPECIES** and using the "superior" offspring for further breeding so that eventually a "superior" species is produced. This process is still taking place today in many fields such as Plant breeding for Flowers and Vegetables and Animal breeding for Racehorses, Pets and domestic farm creatures. It is still normal practice for people who cultivate crops to save seed each year and to be selective in the plants they save seed from in an effort to ensure that the best specimens are retained. This is part of a process known as sustainable agriculture and horticulture.

Not unreasonably efforts have been made to try to increase crop yields, whether it be Plants or Animals. This has led to much research into artificial feeding regimes, which caused the development of artificial fertilizers, and enhanced animal feeds. Unfortunately, this supposed increase in quality and quantity has frequently produced the opposite effect it was meant to and is now making large proportions of the population ask serious questions about food production. The use of artificial feeding and Pesticide use necessary to produce these enhanced yields has meant a much greater input cost is needed and a corresponding increase in "resistant" pests with less natural predators available. At the same time the Plant breeders were producing "Hybrid" seeds which are increasingly expensive and which are unsuitable for saving from one year to the next, so growers are obliged to buy new seed every year. Hybrid seed is seed produced from two widely different varieties and is an attempt to incorporate good characteristics from diverse sources into one new plant. This would be fine if the new "Hybrid" seed performed well but this is not the case. This can be seen in the story of rice grown in Asia. In 1960 there were over 100,000 local strains of rice being grown, each of which was well adapted to its environment, and most were tall varieties with a secondary use for the stems after the grain was harvested. So called superior Hybrid varieties were then introduced which required more inputs and pesticides and which rapidly succumbed to a disease or pest and resulted in the need for another "better" Hybrid.

The situation in Asia now is a long list of failed "superior" Hybrids. As one better characteristic is added another weakness is later discovered and the artificial chemical input is forever increasing. Subsequently, all those traditional Rice varieties which although low cropping were happily surviving with low cost inputs have been lost together with their Genetic code which may have been useful.

To demonstrate the importance of natural genetic diversity and the problems with MONOCULTURE type systems let us look at a fruit, which will be visited again further in the book. APPLES. The United Kingdom has traditionally been one of the leading Apple producers in the world. There is a very long history and the natural development of literally hundreds of varieties. Genetically, the apple tree is designed to perform best over a relatively small range of temperatures, say for argument's sake 45 to 75 degrees Fahrenheit, which is why it suits the United Kingdom. Each of the varieties is particular about the environmental factors it lives in such as light quantity and levels, temperature, moisture, wind and the type of soil. This means that a variety growing in one place happily may not like growing a mere 100 miles either North or South. This partly explains the huge number of varieties that have been grown in this country and thankfully why apple growing is not dominated by only a few varieties. The year 2003 in the United Kingdom was one of record-breaking weather with prolonged periods of high temperatures. This had a deleterious effect on some apples, which were faced with conditions outside their narrow window of ideal growth. Apply this principle of ideal growth to environmental conditions and the problems of Rice growing in Asia become much more easily understood. IT IS NOT VERY POSSIBLE TO MAKE ONE VARIETY OF CROPS FIT ALL CONDITIONS. Yet they are still trying to force Hybrid seed produced in America and Europe onto African farmers whose growing requirements are alien.

To return to present day Genetic Modification and the economy of truth. It has become possible to insert a sequence of DNA (a Gene) into the Genome of an organism. The difference between this and the traditional Plant /Animal breeder is that the Gene inserted comes from **ANOTHER SPECIES,** and would never naturally occur in Nature. It is not therefore surprising that there is a great opposition to this sort of science. Once these organisms are "released" they cannot be retracted and there must be serious doubts about their performance under all the different "local" conditions they will encounter. Surely we should be learning from the problems that have occurred in the growing of Rice and working with Nature as intended.

The process of inserting a new, alien piece of DNA into a Genome is made to sound like a very precise procedure. **Nothing is further from the truth.** When the truth is revealed this whole process becomes even more disturbing. It is not simply a case of "unzipping" the Genome and inserting one new Gene. What is inserted is a "packet" of information containing a large number of DNA components. This whole packet is basically taken into the Genome by a Virus. Viruses are a strange phenomenon in that they can be considered to not be "alive" and not undergo Metabolism. They are simply strands of genetic material in some form of chemical envelope. They reproduce by invading living cells and inserting their strand of genetic material into the cells nucleus. The cell then uses the normal replication process to produce many copies of the virus, which can then disseminate and infect other cells. They are the ultimate parasite.

In genetic modification the packet of information that is inserted can be thought of as a freight train. The Virus part is the engine and the various components are the freight carriages. The genetic modification effect required is obviously something to do with either new or modified Proteins, so some of the freight carriages are related to this production. To produce these proteins requires an obvious controlling element and that is the job of the other freight carriages. On the surface that sounds fine but in practice it is fraught with difficulty.

There is not a lot of control as to where the packet of new information is inserted within the existing Genome. It is not an accurate procedure but mostly hit and miss guesswork. The new packet of information can just as easily get inserted into the middle of an existing Gene as it could get inserted in between Genes. It is quite clear that this is going to have a disruptive effect on the original Genome and that some essential Proteins are no longer going to be coded for. The resultant organism is going to be unstable and perhaps unviable. If the new packet should find itself in a part of the Genome in between Genes, in theory causing no disruption to existing Genes, then this unfortunately is not the end of the matter. The part of the new packet of information, which has a controlling influence on Gene expression of the new Gene, can also affect expression of existing Genes in the original Genome. Yet again producing instability or non-viability of the resultant organism. These effects may not be immediately obvious, hence a need for rigorous long term testing. It therefore takes a great deal of trial and error before the organism with the sought after characteristics are developed.

The problems highlighted are not restricted to the development of these genetically modified organisms but have now led to accepted difficulties outside in the environment. When genetically modified plants are grown in the general environment they hybridize with existing non-genetically modified plants, which are naturally grown. It has been shown that the problems associated with the initial insertion of the new genetic material manifests itself in the naturally occurring hybrids leading to unstable and unviable new plants. This is of course of considerable concern.

There is a human element to this. **The new protein expressed could lead to allergic reactions in some people if consumed!!!**

Reference;   *The Language of the Genes.*
Steve Jones. 1993
ISBN   0 00 654676 5

Chapter 5
VIPEHOLM

Up to now this narrative has hopefully followed a logical sequence in an effort to show how living organisms "work". At this point the description of the mechanics of life is put to one side whilst what appears to be a totally unrelated topic is introduced and this book goes off at a tangent. At first glance the subject of this chapter, although perhaps being of interest, may bear no relation to the rest of the book. In actual fact the principles to be outlined in this chapter are extremely important to the arguments put forward in the rest of the book.

The Vipeholm Study was a long-term piece of research into the factors causing Tooth Decay or to give it its scientific name, CARIES. This research is probably impossible to replicate today because of its ethical implications although its findings were highly important at the time and still remain highly important today. Present day researchers into diseases of the teeth and diet, still have to refer to the findings of the Vipeholm Study. This study took place at the Vipeholm Hospital in Sweden during the years of 1945 to 1953. The Vipeholm Hospital was an institute for the mentally retarded and the experiment carried out on these poor unfortunate people was on dietary control/alteration. Basically, the "patients" of this institute had the level and frequency of their Sucrose intake controlled. Some patients were only allowed Sucrose at low levels at meal times whilst other patients were given higher levels and then other patients were given more frequent doses of Sucrose. After many years it was possible to draw up a correlation between tooth decay and Sucrose consumption and these results, although questionable in their method of production, have been the basis for understanding the process of Caries.

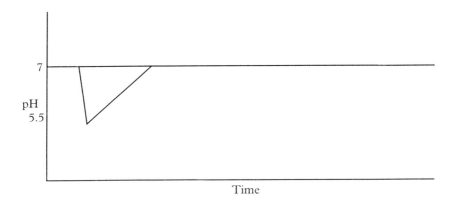

This graph shows what happens in the human mouth following the consumption of the vast majority of food and drink. The resting "pH" of the human mouth is close to 7, which is neutral. Levels beneath pH7 are acidic and levels above pH7 are alkaline. If we return quickly to the breakdown of Glucose, there is a point in the catabolic pathway where Lactic acid can form. In the human mouth, bacteria produce acidic conditions when food or drink is consumed and the end result is what is known as an ACID ATTACK. This acid attack occurs very rapidly and then requires a much longer period of time to return back to the resting level. Tooth decay only tends to take place when the pH of the mouth falls beneath about 5.5, so it can be seen that there is only a short period of time when this occurs. One interesting point that needs to be made is that although the length of time this acid attack is occurring for could be altered due to the length of time food or drink is being consumed, the actual lowering in pH is fairly constant. This means that once an acid attack has occurred it cannot be made much worse although it could be made to last longer.

Now let's produce a graph where a person consumes 3 meals a day.

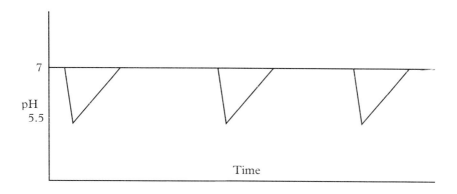

TIME about 12 hours

As can be seen, there are 3 acid attacks and tooth decay can only take place 3 times over a relatively short period of time each time. The process of acidic tooth dissolution, which causes tooth decay, is not a one-way journey and teeth can, if given time, reverse the damage. This "to and fro" demineralization and remineralization takes place continually in human mouths. In this case of only 3 meals a day the likelihood of tooth decay occurring is quite small even if those meals are high in Sucrose/Glucose.

Because the depth of the acid attack cannot be altered appreciably, this means that it would be "safe" to the teeth if those food and drink items, which are known to be particularly "dangerous", were consumed at this point. Therefore, if confectionery is to be consumed it is best done so immediately following a meal. Unfortunately, for a variety of spurious reasons, many people do not consume food and drink restricted to 3 times a day and therefore suffer the consequences. Let us know examine the graph for what unfortunately happens in real life and its effects on the teeth.

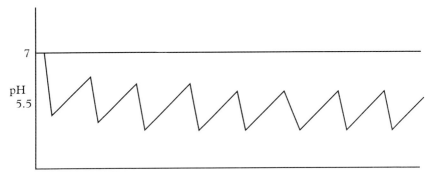

TIME about 12 hours

This graph may be considered "Far fetched" but in actual fact can easily be applied to very large numbers of the population. Remembering that the recovery period back to a resting state is an extended length of time this is what happens. Following an acid attack (breakfast), before the pH of the mouth has returned to its resting state something else is consumed which of course immediately elicits another acid attack. This second acid attack tends to go to a slightly lower pH. Following this second acid attack and before the full recovery period yet more food or drink is consumed with the resultant acid attack. This process continues for most of the day with the result that the mouth never manages to return back to its resting level. Before rejecting this "theory" think about many peoples "normal" day. There are many children who regularly consume packets of confectionery/sweets consisting of little else but sugar, flavouring and colouring OVER A LONG PERIOD OF TIME. They literally can have the confectionery in the mouth for the whole time between two meals and then repeat the process between the next two meals. It is not just children who could be in this situation. Many adults continually "snack" and consume beverages and other drinks high in Sucrose and Glucose.

The result of these continuously acidic mouths is poor oral health and many grossly carious teeth. There will not be a dentist in the country that has not witnessed this terrible state on many occasions and has found they are fighting a losing battle. No sooner has one batch of tooth decay been dealt with, then another fresh amount of tooth decay has occurred. This scenario would NOT be happening if food and drink consumption were restricted to only THREE occasions a day. Looking at many of the nation's mouths this of course is not the case.

As with much of what has been described so far, the Acid Attack Theory and its effects on the teeth has been presented in something of a simplified manner. This does not matter as it puts across the essential problem and its basic solution. As with many aspects of life things are never quite as simple as it first seems and many problems, diseases and unwanted out-comes are multi-factorial in origin. The process of causes of tooth decay is no different and there are other factors that need to be considered. These are; Fluoride, Saliva, and Bacteria/Genetics.

FLUORIDE

The biggest factor in the improvement of tooth decay problems in Britain today has almost certainly been the increase in Fluoride in the environment, principally from toothpaste. Fluoride ions react with the crystals making up tooth enamel and become incorporated within the enamel. The effect of this is the tooth enamel is made more resistant to the acid attacks, which cause tooth decay. Fluoride is also thought to have an inhibiting effect on the bacteria, which produce the tooth dissolving acids. The Fluoride, which is incorporated into the surface of the enamel "leaks" back out and so is only a temporary effect. By adjusting the naturally occurring amount in the water supply to an optimum level, Water fluoridation, the Fluoride is permanently incorporated within teeth AS THEY ARE FORMED. This was thought to give a better ANTI- tooth decay effect although more recent work has confused this issue.

Simple Fluoride toothpaste is definitely a great weapon in fighting the tooth decay problem.

SALIVA

Saliva has many essential functions especially in protecting the teeth from tooth decay. Whilst it may be thought of as simply a lubricant to aid in chewing and swallowing there are many other properties.

The saliva contains the necessary ions, which help repair the teeth following acid dissolution of tooth surfaces. There is hence a reversal of any acid attack damage that may have occurred.

A very important role is that of what is known as a BUFFERING agent. The saliva neutralizes and holds in check the acids, which are formed following the consumption of food and drink. It is responsible for restricting the acid attack spike and for hastening the recovery of the pH back to its resting level. It is this property, which has led to the somewhat silly claims made by the chewing gum producers, who now make oral health statements. The chewing of gum after a meal merely increases the flow of saliva. This increased saliva flow will increase the Buffering action and therefore decrease the recovery period. This decrease in recovery period is only of a small amount and is probably not significant BUT it has been "jumped on" by the chewing gum producers as a marketing ploy. The essential effect of saliva's buffering action is seen by all dentists in those patients who have decreased saliva flow due to either the natural reduction that can occur in aging or those who have had Radiotherapy around the head. In these circumstances it is noted that the rate of tooth decay starts to rise and new carious cavities are formed, often in unconventional places. This is obviously most disconcerting for the patient as besides suffering the inconvenience of having a "dry mouth", which possibly becomes sore through lack of lubrication, they also find themselves the recipients of more tooth restorations.

BACTERIA/GENETICS

Over the last few years there have been considerable strides forward in discovery about the bacterial make-up of the human mouth. The number of bacterial species now cultivated from the human mouth now stands at over "500" and the actual number of millions of bacteria living in the human mouth appears unresolvable. If you were to work out the number of different permutations that this could produce, the figure would be almost infinite (for all intents and purposes). This means there have almost certainly never been two humans with the same bacterial make-up in their mouths. The bacteria present are probably largely determined by those acquired very early in life with a big input from the parents. All of the bacteria in the mouth will be living in a state of ecological balance. This means no one species will tend to become dominant as there are plenty of other species keeping "rogues" in their place. Thus, the concept of beneficial bacteria.

Some bacteria will be more aggressive than others and different mouths will have differing types of bacteria. If a person is unlucky, then they could acquire a bacterial make-up, which contains the more aggressive types of bacteria. This means that if they acquired the aggressive bacteria that were responsible for lactic acid production and hence tooth caries then they would be more at risk of tooth decay. This goes a long way to explaining how different people can have different experiences of tooth decay whilst consuming similar diets. If you have mild bacteria then you may be relatively resistant to tooth decay but, if you have aggressive bacteria then it will take relatively little to cause tooth cavities.

Quite obviously the mix of Dietary habits, Fluoride, Saliva properties and Bacterial make-up are all going to have an effect on Caries experience in any individual. BUT, the most important factor and the one which individuals have most control over is their frequency of food and drink consumption.

EROSION

In traditional teaching of Dental Undergraduate Students, besides the destructive tooth loss known as caries there were three other methods of tooth tissue loss listed. These were ATTRITION, ABRASION and EROSION. Attrition is the wear on teeth due to the natural process of mastication and can simply be thought of as wear to the chewing and biting surfaces. Abrasion was wear to the lateral surfaces of teeth and was thought to be due to incorrect, over forceful toothbrushing. It was the reason for the development of "sensitive formula toothpastes". Erosion was considered a relatively rare event caused by external acid attack to the teeth. Times have changed and the dental profession have now got a far better idea of what happens in the human mouth with the result that Dental Erosion has become far more important and Dental abrasion is far better understood. What has perhaps surprised many is that the VIPEHOLM STUDY has gained renewed importance.

The Dental profession have now learnt most of what there is to learn about the process and dietary causes of CARIES. Also, with the reduction in tooth decay, which has occurred, probably due to Fluoride, there is less emphasis on the treatment of tooth decay. As it happens a new problem has occurred and subsequently more understanding of what happens in the human mouth has developed. Instead of teenagers presenting with problems of tooth decay, they are now turning up with painful mouths due to the process of Dental Erosion. This problem has probably always been present at a low level BUT changes in diet combined with a reduction in tooth decay have made it far more noticeable. Returning to VIPEHOLM, it is apparent that teeth will "dissolve" when the pH of the mouth falls beneath 5.5, and this fact is vital to explaining what is presently being seen.

Recent research has shown that children appear to fall into two groups regarding their drinking habits. One group of children get their liquid intake from water, and this includes Tea, Coffee, and Milk and dilute squash. The other group of children do not get their liquid intake from water so quite obviously it must come elsewhere. This group of children get their liquid intake from "carbonated Drinks". These carbonated drinks usually contain; Carbonic acid, Phosphoric acid and Citric acid and consequently they have low pH values. (pH values can be less than 4). Whilst it would be acceptable for the occasional consumption of these drinks, unfortunately in many cases they are drunk frequently over a prolonged period of time and also held in the mouth before swallowing.

The end result is the teeth are bathed in a highly acidic solution for a long period of time with dire consequences. The surface of the teeth is literally dissolved away!!! Not surprisingly the teeth become sensitive and it is a difficult restorative problem for the treating dentist. There also appears to be a serious side effect to this, which has not as yet been resolved;

THE BUFFERING EFFECT OF THE SALIVA IS REDUCED IN THESE EROSIVE INDIVIDUALS.

The effect of this is obvious. The mouth can no longer protect itself from the harmful results of acid attacks with this leading to an increased risk of tooth decay. As yet the research has not been carried out to determine whether the changes in saliva are permanent and the mode of operation, which causes this apparent change.

CONCLUSIONS AND ASIDES

Looking at VIPEHOLM afresh the dental profession have come to a number of conclusions, which reverse previous advice and help explain other observations. The effect of the "acid attack" is to alter the surface layers of teeth, and here we need to think in highly magnified, microscopic terms. This alteration of the surface layer is negated if the teeth are given sufficient time to recover and return to the normal resting state. BUT, if something interferes with this recovery process then permanent harm could occur. THUS;

TOOTHBRUSHING SHOULD NOT TAKE PLACE WITHIN AN HOUR OF CONSUMING FOOD OR DRINK.

This of course is contrary to what has been normal advice and practice for many years. People are taught to clean their teeth immediately after breakfast, which is the wrong thing to do. This explains the phenomenon of what was called Dental Abrasion .It was in fact abrasion of ERODED teeth and not merely incorrect toothbrushing technique.

Another important point needs to be made which many people find difficult to comprehend.

THE PURPOSE OF CLEANING TEETH IS TO KEEP THE GUMS HEALTHY AND PREVENT PERIODONTAL DISEASE. IT IS NOT TO PREVENT TOOTH DECAY.

Tooth decay is related to diet. Toothbrushing will only have a beneficial effect by introducing Fluoride into the oral environment.

Having rubbished the use of chewing gum to reverse the effects of an acid attack the question has to be asked, "can anything help to reverse the process"? There are two things, which are known to have a beneficial effect, CHEESE and plain salted peanuts. They have the following effect on the pH of the mouth.

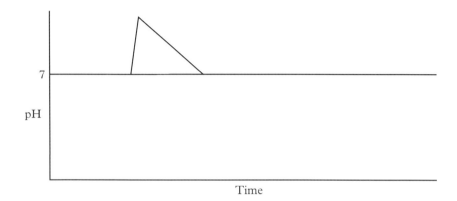

Eating cheese after a meal is a traditional event. Completely by accident, there is a sound scientific basis to this tradition. If a meal is finished with cheese then a very beneficial effect on the associated acid attack can occur and hence protection from possible tooth decay. This also means that cheese (and plain salted peanuts) is a "safe" food to eat in between meals, as it will not cause an acid attack. Later on there will be discussion about good and bad diet and some of the "daft and incorrect" ideas will be commented on. It is nonsense to make the sweeping statement that cheese and dairy products are "bad" for you. This is not the case. Assuming an element of moderation, no harm will occur by eating cheese either before, during, after or between meals! The question of plain salted peanuts is one of those conundrums where it may be difficult to give a clear answer.

Putting all the previous facts of this chapter together we are now in the position to make a number of recommendations, especially regarding the habits of schools. It has become a so-called "good practice" for schools to be giving children fruit at break-times between breakfast and lunch. This is ill thought out nonsense. Fruit is full of sugar and it is no different to that white granular substance bought in packets even though it is "natural". There is no benefit to a child eating fruit between meals! If schools insist on allowing anything other than water at break-times then the only safe item would be a lump of cheese!

An even worse phenomenon is the common practice of placing "vending machines" within schools. Virtually all the merchandise from these vending machines contain large proportions of sugar which the children then consume over an extended period of time between meals. Much of the drinks from these machines are also highly acidic, just to compound the damage .It all adds up to the development of poor dietary habits, which perhaps become permanent and a compromised lifestyle.

Chapter 6
DIET AND NUTRITION
(Balance and Moderation)

Earlier on the subject of the final of the Olympic games 100 metres was raised to demonstrate energy and muscle usage. Let us return briefly to that image now as a very important point can be made. Are any of those runners fat, overweight or Obese? Indeed, are any of the fit athletes participating in sports and games an example of fat or overweight people? The answer to these questions has to be a loud and resounding NO.

The point being made should be quite obvious. There is a huge, NONSENSICAL business in the United Kingdom, giving much BAD ADVICE, regarding diet and weight-loss. It would not be too strong a comment to say that much of this business could be viewed as fraudulent! Many, many people are spending a great deal of time and money, pursuing ridiculous eating habits and being taken in by a series of unqualified, uneducated Quacks, "Experts", Life-style gurus etc, etc. The following is a SCIENTIFIC and FACTUAL account of the need for, and good practice of, diet and nutrition. There are NO fads, fancies, ill-informed opinion or pseudo-science.

WASTE

This is going to appear to be a strange place to start the subject of diet and nutrition but in fact as will be seen is entirely logical. People have got the wrong idea about the topic of bowel excrement, known scientifically as FAECES. It is generally thought that faeces are waste from the body's metabolism. This is not the case. Faeces are made up of; undigested food, non-digestible food, dead and alive bacteria and dead cells. The intestinal system does not allow for the removal of excess food intake beyond the body's needs. Faeces have played no part in the actual working of an organism. To try to ensure understanding of this point and its relationship to the word "Waste" let us equate it to the purchase of a new, large kitchen appliance. The new appliance comes in a large cardboard box with polystyrene packaging. We throw the cardboard box and packaging away as it plays NO PART in the functioning of the new appliance. Faeces are like the unwanted packaging of our food intake.

Absorption of food is a one-way process from the intestinal tract. Food cannot pass backward and forward across the intestinal membrane. In place of the word food, let us instead use the word "CALORIE". What the above now means is that if Calories are consumed then they are going to be absorbed, whether the body needs them or not. Calories cannot be rejected or passed back out of the body into the alimentary canal. For Calories to be absorbed the process of digestion has to be utilized and this may not be 100% efficient. Therefore, someone who consumes a "Whole-Food", unprocessed diet may not extract all the Calories taken in and they will be ejected in the Faeces. On the other hand, someone who takes in Calories from processed food (and drink) will absorb all of them much more readily as they are digested more easily.

Therefore;
CALORIES THAT ARE TAKEN IN
ARE GOING TO STAY IN.

If faeces are not waste from metabolism, how is metabolic waste dealt with? The answer is two systems, the lungs and the kidneys. If you go back to the Krebs, Citric acid or TCA cycle, it is for the conversion of small organic molecules into energy and "Carbon Dioxide". The carbon dioxide is transported in the bloodstream to the lungs where it is exhaled into the external environment. Other small molecules, which are left over from metabolism, are filtered from the bloodstream by the kidneys and excreted in the urine. Urine can hence be viewed as "true waste". Returning to the beginning of this book and the construction of organic molecules there are four main elements involved; Carbon, Hydrogen, Oxygen and Nitrogen. The first three elements are excreted as carbon dioxide and water. The Nitrogen, mostly from amino acids derived from proteins, is excreted in the urine in the form of Urea.

There is thus no method for the body to get rid of Calories other than the production of "Energy". The amount of "Energy" required on a daily basis will be discussed shortly but it should be obvious that we cannot simply produce more "Energy" than the body needs. Therefore, any excess Calories taken in have to go somewhere as storage and the body deals with this by converting Calories into "FAT".

CALORIES AND BASAL METABOLIC RATE

As was intimated at the beginning of this chapter this account is based on proven scientific research and data. Therefore, and perhaps unfortunately for some, this section by necessity has a large amount of mathematics. It is vitally important to the understanding of the rest of the chapter.

Firstly nomenclature.

1 Calorie = 1 Kilo-calorie = 1000 calories = 4186 joules

    1 Calorie   is the heat required to raise the temperature of 1 Kilo-gram of water 1degree Celsius

    & 1 calorie is the hear required to raise the temperature of 1 gram of water 1 degree Celsius

1 Kilowatt-hour = 860 Calories   1 Horsepower-hour = 641 Calories

Don't be taken in by the latest food manufacturer "gimmick". By playing around with the units and quoting energy content in "mega-joules" (mj) on the packaging it can appear to those of us used to the word "calorie" that there is less energy present. This is simply a deliberate attempt to confuse.

Food Calories;

Oxygen is needed for the catabolism of food and we get the following figures.

1 gram of carbohydrate + 820 ml Oxygen = 4.1 Calories

1 gram of fat   + 1980 ml Oxygen = 9.3 Calories

1 gram of protein   = 4   Calories

These figures show that;

For Carbohydrate 1 Litre of Oxygen   = 5.4 Calories

For Fat   1 Litre of Oxygen   = 4.4 Calories

This provides us with a VITALLY important piece of information;

OXYGEN USAGE EQUATES TO CALORIE USAGE

Lets quickly go back to the Olympic games. All these fit athletes have one thing in common, THEY ALL HAVE HIGH OXYGEN USAGE. This means they burn a lot of Calories.

Another important concept linked to Calories is Basal Metabolic Rate. This is the number of Calories that need to be used just to keep our bodies ticking over and can be thought of as a figure for the number of Calories used whilst lying relatively motionless in bed either per hour or per day. The Basal Metabolic Rate is related to the Body Surface Area and is measured in Calories per square metre of surface area per hour.

As an average;
BMR for man   = 40 Calories per m2 per hour
BMR for woman = 37 Calories per m2 per hour

This is for people of about 20 years of age.

For a man;
Height 175 cms, Weight 67 Kg = 70 Calories per hour
    (5' 9")   (10.5 stone)

This equates to about 1730 Calories per day

If we add about 1000 Calories for activity we get approximately 2800 Calories per day.

REMEMBER THIS FIGURE.

Basal Metabolic Rate varies per square
metre in a number of ways;

1. Sex
2. Age group. Higher in growing children. Less in elderly.
3. Fitness Levels. Higher in fitter people.
4. External temperature. Warmer climate lower BMR
5. Nutrition Levels. Lower in starvation conditions
6. Disease. If body temperature rises by 1 degree Fahrenheit then BMR rises by 7%.

An extremely important point comes out of this data;

IF CALORIE INTAKE IS LESS THAN BASAL METABOLIC RATE, THEN THE BASAL METABOLIC RATE WILL FALL AND READJUST.

All of those people on diets MUST be aware of the above statement and those attending "dieting clubs" could be in a fraudulent situation!

There are hence two ways that Calorie usage can be increased;

Increase work or increase Basal Metabolic Rate

TO INCREASE BASAL METABOLIC RATE THEN OXYGEN CONSUMPTION NEEDS TO BE INCREASED AND THIS IS ACHIEVED BY INCREASE IN "EXERCISE" and hence Fitness levels.

It should now be obvious that Calorie needs vary from individual to individual depending upon work levels and Basal Metabolic Rate. The range for daily Calorie needs is; 2250 - -> above 5000.

The Basal Metabolic Rate is linked to the Thyroid gland, which is found in the neck. The Thyroid gland secretes hormones and a reduction in these hormones can cause the Basal Metabolic Rate to fall and lead to a disease called Myxoedema. An increase in Thyroid hormone secretion causes the disease process known as Thyrotoxicosis and this leads to an increase in Basal Metabolic Rate.

CALORIES AND FOOD INTAKE

Knowing that the average Calorie requirements are of the order of about 2500 per day it should now be possible to link this to food substances and get some idea as to how much food needs to be consumed. As was mentioned earlier, different foods have different Calorific values when mixed with Oxygen and it is worth repeating those values;

1 gram Carbohydrate = 4.1 Calorie
1 gram Fat   = 9.3 Calorie
1 gram Protein   = 4.0 Calorie

About 90% of our energy needs traditionally comes from a mixture of Carbohydrate and Fat, with the 10% Protein mostly used for growth, repair and new tissue. If the diet includes more Protein then it will be used for energy purposes.

One teaspoon of sugar is about 10 grams of carbohydrate, which equates to about 40 Calories. Let us apply this to soft drinks and beverages, keeping in mind the overall Calorie needs. How many cups of Tea and Coffee are consumed by the average person each day? Let us say 5 per day and let us assume that for many people 2 teaspoons of sugar are used each time. This would equate to 400 Calories per day or about one sixth of the total Calorie needs. Now let's consider canned soft drinks, which have become the daily source of liquid intake for many people, especially children. Most of these cans of drink contain the equivalent of between 7 and 10 teaspoons of sugar, about 300-400 Calories. Is it any wonder that some children are suffering from Obesity when they are sometimes consuming perhaps 5 cans a day! This could be over 60% of their daily Calorie needs. Besides the Calories taken in via these drinks, the drinks are often taken with snacks and confectionery. Thus, one small biscuit amounts to above 20 Calories, one packet of crisps or similar amounts to about 150 Calories and a chocolate bar is of the order of 150 - - - - 400 Calories. It would not take many "high Calorie" chocolate bars to make up a very big percentage of daily Calorie needs. Picture now the scene in many schools and offices in the United Kingdom. It would be very easy to find people consuming 1000 Calories from snacks and drinks taken BETWEEN meals. Is it any wonder that so many people are having problems with being over-weight?

Below is a small list of some food products with approximate figures for Calories. It is by no means strictly accurate but this is not important, as it is simply to give a rough idea. The figures given are Calories per 100 grams (about 3 ounces)

Bread	200	Potato crisps	500
Bacon	375	Breakfast cereal	300-400
Potato	100-250	Chocolate bars	150-400
Cheese	300	Pot Noodle	400 per pack
Meat	150-300	Biscuits	300-400
Fresh Fish	100-150	Mayonnaise	400-700
Peas	50	Butter	700
Apple	45	Onion Rings	200
Banana	60	Tomato ketchup	125
Egg	150	Pasta	300
Milk	70	Broccoli	15
Brussel Sprouts	15	Cabbage	15

The above shows that many of those food items classed as "snacks or novelties" are high in Calories compared to "basic" food products and they are all processed foods. This means their Calories are readily absorbed from the alimentary tract and there is very little protein, vitamins or essential minerals.

Let us now turn our attention to the subject of so called "Fast Food". This "Fast Food" commonly is a mixture of some form of reconstituted grilled meat, high in fat, within a bread roll served with French fried potatoes (chips) and a soft drink. The example used will be taken from the North American experience, where there is now a severe problem with Obesity. The history of McDonalds will be used showing the effects of economic pressure and its attempts to consolidate its market share. In the 1960's the standard meal served amounted to about 500 Calories. The standard portion of fries was about 200 Calories. By severely cutting and controlling costs, the portions being offered increased without increase in cost to the consumer. The end result is the standard meal now being offered (fries, burger and drink) amounts to about 1500 Calories! What has happened, across the board, is that over a 40-year period the Calorific content has increased by about 300%. Bearing in mind normal Calorie needs then one standard McDonalds meal contributes about 60%!

To demonstrate how potentially damaging this can be let us look at some incontrovertible facts associated with the consumption of this "fast meal". The rate of Calorie intake is of the order of 200-250 per minute. Compare this with expenditure. The maximum rate of aerobic energy expenditure is of the order of 25 Calories per minute and over the course of 24 hours the average person uses 1.5 Calories per minute. It can be seen therefore, that a very large number of Calories are taken on board VERY rapidly. The Stomach is a very interesting organ whose function is far more complex than most people realize. The stomach will deal with different foods at different rates and therefore, those foods requiring more digestive action will remain in the stomach longer than those needing less digestive action. "Fast food" by its very nature is highly processed and requires little digestive action before it is ready for absorption by the small intestine. What happens is the fast food and drink rapidly pass through the stomach into the small intestine where it quickly is taken up by the body and the blood stream is flooded by broken down food products, GLUCOSE. The body's response to the high level of Glucose in the blood is to release high levels of the hormone, INSULIN. It has been shown that excessive levels of Insulin are not good for us and it is thought that continuous high level "bursts" of Insulin in this manner could be responsible for the development of Diabetes. Whilst the body of course is designed to release Insulin following a meal in response to elevated blood Glucose, with "normal" unprocessed carbohydrate intake the rate of Glucose entering the bloodstream is slower. The Insulin is released in a more controlled, lower level manner.

A further point is raised from the above. The fast food has exited the stomach much faster than a more traditional diet and consequently it does not engender a great feeling of "fullness", known scientifically as SATIETY. A traditional meal of balanced proportions of carbohydrate, fat and protein, with unprocessed food products will need far more digestive action and hence will remain in the stomach for longer. The effect is to give the feeling of SATIETY and hence feeding will tend to cease. This is a very important principle and can be easily summed up by the following;

IT IS DIFFICULT TO GET OVERWEIGHT ON NON-PROCESSED FOOD AS ITS NATURAL BULK FILLS US UP.

Much of the increase in Calories can be put down to two developments in the early 1970's. First there was the development of High Fructose Corn Syrup "HFCS" from corn which was of course readily available and cheap in North America. "HFCS" was 6 times sweeter than cane sugar and replaced sucrose in many products. One result of this technology was a change in carbonated drinks. The vast majority of carbonated drinks are now simply mixtures of "HFCS" and carbonated water with different flavourings to denote different brands. The second development was the technology to purify "Palm Oil" so that it could be used for frying and the production of "Ready Meals". Palm Oil was again extremely cheap and readily available. It is a very stable but highly saturated Fat.

Unfortunately, both "HFCS" and Palm Oil have caused health problems and controversy. "HFCS" consumption increase has matched the increase in Obesity in society. Its biochemistry within the mammalian body is complicated but it has been shown that there is a rise in Triglycerides in the bloodstream, which damages arteries and adds to the problem of coronary heart disease. Although Fructose is very very closely related to Glucose it is not metabolized in the same way and it is thought that Fructose is immediately converted to Fat by the liver. High calorific Fructose therefore, increases fat production, known as Lipogenesis, and it also makes mammalian cells resistant to the effects of Insulin. This results in Diabetes. Palm Oil has also been shown to produce Insulin resistance and hence a rise in Diabetes incidence.

There has been an unequivocal rise in both Obesity and Diabetes in much of the "Western" world, which almost certainly is due to Calorific intake being in excess of the body's needs, and both "HFCS" and Palm Oil are implicated. The blood vessel damage related to Diabetes leads to nerve damage, causing numbness and gangrene and also blindness from damaged retinal blood vessels. Diabetes also causes muscle atrophy, cirrhosis of the liver, gallstones and problems with sex hormones. Obesity leads to coronary heart disease, hypertension, and strokes and puts great strain on the skeleton leading to joint problems.

CHILDRENS DIET COMPARISONS

In June 2000, the United Kingdom published a report on the national diet and nutrition of 4-18 year old children. It was possible to compare the findings with a previous survey carried out in 1983. Some of the findings were as follows;

15-18 year old girls drank two thirds more fizzy drinks than milk and they ate 4 times as much sweets and chocolates than leafy green vegetables.

Boys eat 4 times as many biscuits as leafy green vegetables.

The most common foods eaten by over 80% of children were; white bread, savory snacks, potato chips (fries), biscuits, potatoes, and chocolate.

Vegetable eating was not a strong characteristic.

Three-quarters of children drank carbonated drinks regularly.

Energy intakes were LOWER than the 1983 survey BUT body size had INCREASED. This showed energy needs were lower BUT there was a decrease in activity/exercise.

Sugar intake was higher than recommended.

"The total amount of Calories derived from sugar should be less than 10% of total daily intake of Calories".

The vitamin A intakes were lower than recommended. (low vegetable intake)

In older children, the mineral intake was below recommended levels.

13% of 11-18 year olds had a poor vitamin D status. (lack of sunlight)

Activity levels were low. (only 1-6% cycled to school)

The diets of children growing up in the 1950's have been broadly compared to present day children. Calorie intake in the 1950's was 20% higher but the children were smaller, fitter and less fat. They took much more exercise and their homes were not so well heated. **Their Basal Metabolic Rate was higher!** Their diet had much less sugar and there were far fewer fizzy drinks so there was a much lower consumption of "Empty" Calories. Today's children spend their time indoors. 65% have televisions in their bedrooms. They are eating less than 2 portions of fruit and vegetables per day (recommended level is 5 portions per day) and there are signs of malnourishment and vitamin deficiencies.

In 2001, Epidemiologists at the University of Minnesota carried out a survey of 5000 teenage boys concerning their daily Calorie intake. This is their findings;

No fast food was eaten	1952 Calories daily
Fast food eaten 1-2 times per week	2192 Calories daily
Fast food eaten 3 and over per week	2752 Calories daily

FAST FOOD IS FINE AS AN OCCASIONAL TREAT.
No more than once per week.

DIETARY NONSENSE

As has already been intimated the subject of diet and nutrition seems to be full of falsehoods and misconceptions, even with those closely working with it. The area of food and health is filled with Quacks, Cranks and purveyors of Pseudoscience who are uneducated, untrained and unqualified. There is a large body of people, carrying out a job, which frankly does not exist, advising other people on how they should lead their lives. These "Gurus" have a lack of basic knowledge and science in their chosen "field". They are completely unqualified and worming their way into all aspects of life. Even the present Prime Minster of the

United Kingdom and his family have employed, and been taken in by one of these totally unqualified **"Advisers"**.

Unfortunately, many of the "professional" and honest, hard working people who work in diet and nutrition appear to lack the essential, background training in human biochemistry and hence offer advice which may be flawed. Even the Medical Profession readily admits that General Medical Practitioners are not given proper training in the area of Diet and Nutrition. The result is General Practitioners are at something of a disadvantage as they try to deal with the "Ticking Time Bomb" of OBESITY. It is all very well expecting the Medical Profession to treat the after effects of Diabetes and Obesity but really efforts should be made to prevent it occurring which means giving effective advice.

One of the things, which graphically illustrate the previous two paragraphs, is the commonly expressed saying "THE PACE OF MODERN LIFE". This is complete and utter NONSENSE. There is NO pace of modern life. This expression is probably a marketing ploy generated initially by the food manufacturing industry together with the supermarkets. It is a concept promulgated by the food industry to ensure that the population continues to buy the processed, so called convenience, frozen and ready meals. The present population, in comparison to 40 years ago, works far shorter hours and probably easier hours. The only harder bit is the curse of travelling and the motorcar. Daily life is dominated by the over-used and abused Computer, which is a so-called "Labour saving device"!! The present population has far more leisure time compared to 40 years ago. "The pace of modern life" is simply an excuse for laziness. It is the reason used to ensure a daily fix of "Soap Operas". It is to ensure that at least 5 hours of television is fitted in every day and the development of a nation of "Couch Potatoes"!!

What the nation needs is to go back to proper cooking with proper family meals and not the "self service cafeteria" type lifestyle, which has become accepted. The Supermarkets need to be full of freshly grown and picked LOCAL produce. Not full of processed food.

To illustrate the points made so far in this section the following is a quote from a recently released document. In November 2003 a document was released titled; A Leaner Fitter Future. This is a dossier compiled of the opinions from nearly 30 organizations regarding overweight children. It is being jointly led by The Association for the Study of Obesity (ASO) and the quote is by Dr Susan JEBB the chairperson of ASO.

"This is the first attempt to focus the views of such a diverse group of relevant stakeholders. Nearly all stakeholders agree that the causes of obesity are multi-factorial, but rooted in contemporary western diets and lifestyles - too sedentary for some, but with the pace and demands of modern life leaving little time for healthy diets and exercise, too fast for others."

WHAT A TRULY STUPID AND IDIOTIC STATEMENT.

This is exactly what was meant when criticizing people who are working in the field of diet and nutrition. Dr Jebb really should have known better unless perhaps her background is not food, diet or nutrition and she is a political figurehead. Statements like this are simply encouraging people to find an excuse for their dietary habits. There are probably only a fraction of 1% of people who find themselves in a position of work that come anywhere near Dr Jebb's statement. What percentage of the population are deemed overweight or Obese? Certainly NOT due to the pace of modern life.

There is another misconception freely touted that the big culprit is FAT. This is not the case. That is not to say that Fat is good for you or that some people should not make an effort to control their fat intake. Perspectives have been lost and Fat is incorrectly being made the scapegoat. The culprit is "CALORIES". The issue of Fat content is yet again being used as a marketing ploy by the food manufacturers and supermarkets to sell their produce. One supermarket has recently blatantly made a big issue of attaching prominent labels on some of its goods highlighting the fat content. This was of course for the benefit and health of its customers. RUBBISH! This was done in an effort to "put one over on the opposition", attract more customers and to sell more of another type of somewhat "flawed" food produce. The problem with Fat would largely go away if what was stated earlier took place. If people went back to cooking fresh, UNPROCESSED, food for themselves whilst acknowledging the place of unsaturated fats and things like Olive Oil, the issue of Fat would mostly disappear.

The problem with Fat is its high usage in Fast foods, frozen and chilled ready meals, savory snacks and other processed foods. Fat is necessary in our diets and its high usage in processed foods is needed to make them palatable. In an effort to ensure sales of food products the food manufacturers have been tinkering with the ingredients and substituting some of the Fats with other things. The sort of things used is plant-based starches and gums and animal based proteins both of which are made into emulsions and gels to improve food texture. There has also been an effort to replace saturated fats with fats of a slightly lower calorific value. These food products are then advertised as "REDUCED FAT FOOD". In most instances these reduced fat foods have THE SAME NUMBER OF CALORIES! Virtually all processed food also, by necessity, has large amounts of sugar, which adds to the high Calorie content.

Again, these foods would not be palatable/edible without the high sugar content. The food manufacturers have kept up their record when labeling these products by making what may be construed as misleading claims such as "NO ADDED SUGAR". There is already an excessive amount due to the manufacturing process.

The result of all of these processed foods is people are consuming a lot of readily absorbed Calories, sometimes called "empty" Calories, which they do not need. These are exactly the food products, which rapidly pass through the stomach with little need for digestion and hence get rapidly absorbed by the small intestine. The problem with processed foods is there is a lack of "bulk" and this may lead to having to consume more food to satisfy. At least with the traditional British fast food of "Fish and Chips" there is a large quantity of bulky fried potatoes besides the advantage of eating Fish and the food being of an unprocessed nature. It was probably much lower in Calories than the standard McDonalds meal mentioned earlier and had far fewer additives as well.

Another misconception regarding Fat is the criticism leveled at Milk and Cheese. Cheese always seems to be a target with efforts from **"? Who knows"** to turn it into a bland, sterile, tasteless product. LEAVE IT ALONE. It is good for you as long as it is not seriously over-indulged. It is one of our great natural food products like carrots and Brussels sprouts!

DIETING MAKES YOU FAT

It is a well-known fact that for those people who go on a diet, they quickly return to their former self when they finish their diet. They find themselves on a continuous "roller coaster" of fluctuating weight levels. The title of this section has been known for over 30 years but the dieting and weight-watching industries have kept very quiet about it. Earlier on it was stated that possibly the conduct of the dieting industry and clubs etc could almost be viewed as fraudulent. There is obviously a huge and profitable industry at work here who not unnaturally wants to protect their interest. Bearing in mind everything that has gone previously in this book and particularly the earlier facts of this chapter let us put our cards on the table;

THE ONLY WAY TO CONSISTENTLY, EFFICIENTLY AND PERMANENTLY LOSE WEIGHT IS TO RAISE THE BASAL METABOLIC RATE WHILST CONTROLLING THE CALORIE INTAKE.

This is not new. It is not "rocket science". You do not need special food products, as it will occur with "normal" food. You do not need special diets. You do not need to join a club. You do not need to read special magazines.
But,

The only way to raise Basal Metabolic Rate is to EXERCISE.

Now here is the really shocking part. If you go on a lowered Calorie diet without increasing exercise levels; you **lower your Basal Metabolic Rate.**

Is it now any wonder that the dieting industry can be accused of being fraudulent!

Let us go through the typical dieting process. You are overweight and therefore join a dieting club. Basal Metabolic Rate is say 1600 Calories per day and you are put on a regime of Calorie intake of 2000 per day. Your body needs 1000 Calories per day for general activity, so you need 2600 Calories per day, which means you are 600 Calories short per day. Fine, you will find these 600 Calories from your fat reserves and lose weight, or so you are told. WRONG. Firstly your fat reserves are not mobilized so easily and your initial weight loss will come from other sources. Secondly your Basal Metabolic Rate will reduce to compensate for the reduction in Calorie intake. Eventually a status quo will be reached and you will slowly lose weight. Sounds pretty grim and an unattractive lifestyle.

Unfortunately the worst is yet to come. After some time you reach your desired conclusion and come off the diet. Applause all round. Your Basal Metabolic Rate is now set at 1300 Calories per day and your normal dietary intake has gone up to 2600 Calories per day. You still need 1000 Calories for normal activity so there is an excess of 300 Calories per day. The excess Calories are laid down into your fat reserves. **DIETING MAKES YOU FAT.** It has been shown that you can in fact change the proportions of the make up of your body and increase the overall percentage of Fat. And what is the overall end result? Six months later you are overweight again and go on a diet!!!!!!! Is this not a common scenario? The dieting industry knows all this but keeps strangely quiet.

There is of course another, better, more scientific way of losing weight, which has the advantage of increasing overall health, fitness and life span. There are two important facts;

1. Increasing Oxygen consumption, through exercise and becoming fitter, naturally burns more Calories throughout the day.

2. It takes 20 minutes of Aerobic exercise before the body burns fat. It uses carbohydrate reserves first.

Therefore, without changing Calorie consumption, if you were to take more exercise and raise your Basal Metabolic Rate you would lose weight in a more consistent and permanent manner. To many people perhaps this does not seem very appealing but the exercise can be relatively gentle. What is important is that the heart rate has to be increased for a continuous period of time and therefore the exercise needed has to be of a prolonged steady nature. Therefore, in rising order of benefit; continuous prolonged walking, prolonged continuous swimming, cycling, aerobic exercise classes and probably the best a 3-mile continuous run (jogging). Things like playing Squash are not considered very helpful. There is nothing here which requires anything other than a small cultural change, back to 40 years ago and the use of sports playing fields in schools.

Reference has been made to terms such as pseudo-science. There is no quirky answer to the question of overweight and dieting and the following is an explanation of a recent phenomenon. When protein is consumed there is an increase in energy usage and more heat is generated. Possibly this is due to a change within Mitochondria where the Electron Transport Chain is "decoupled" and instead of ATP production heat is generated. BUT, this effect is very small and not significant. Unfortunately, this small effect was picked up on and misinterpreted by a flawed scientist who thought it was a way of losing weight. The scientist died of Obesity ! In fact the reason why this suspect diet has an effect is quite simple and has already been explained earlier in the chapter. A high protein diet produces a state of SATIETY more quickly than one containing balanced proportions. Therefore, **"less food/calories are ingested"** and the effect is simply a calorie-controlled diet !!

CALORIE RESTRICTION. EXTENDED LIFESPAN

It has become well established that reducing food intake and hence Calorie restriction extends the lifespan in a wide range of species, in what are known as "lower" life forms. The biochemistry is complicated but the restriction in Calories appears to be associated with a change in metabolism and a change in Oxygen consumption. It is also associated with an increased production of an enzyme, via DNA, called SIRTUIN.

The SIRTUIN together with the change in Oxygen consumption affects the intracellular concentration of a molecule intimately involved in metabolism, especially in catabolism in the Krebs or TCA cycle.

SIRTUIN production is stimulated by molecules called polyphenols, which are found in plants and fruit. One of the better-known polyphenols is RESVERATROL, which is abundant in Red Wine. This is one of the reasons for the health claims associated with the drinking of red wine. Unfortunately, the mode of action and dosage required of Resveratrol is complicated and its beneficial effects cannot be gained simply by "popping a pill".

What the above does show is yet another health benefit from a diet whose Calorie intake is better matched to Calorie needs combined with Oxygen consumption, which is related to fitness and Basal Metabolic Rate. It would appear that not only would a sensible diet and Calorie consumption reduce the likelihood of developing chronic diseases such as coronary heart disease, strokes, diabetes, cancer and skeletal disorders but also it will also naturally extend lifespan. To achieve this, as will be shown shortly, does not mean living like a celibate, vegetarian monk but in fact can mean eating a varied, flavoursome and even gourmet like diet.

Reference;   Howitz et al. NATURE 425, 191-196 (2003)

VIPEHOLM REVISITED

Earlier on the subject of Vipeholm was introduced and although it may have been interesting it may not appeared to have any relevance to the rest of this book. In actual fact it proposes a theory, which has great relevance to the habits of good diet and hence good health. If, for the health of one part of the alimentary tract a proposal is made then that proposal probably applies to the rest of the alimentary tract. The proposal being made is that; Calories **should only be consumed 3 times per day.**

If Calories are only consumed at 3 times during the day then this will go a long way to developing a good habit and a Calorie controlled diet. It will instill the discipline of eating proper meals at set mealtimes, a good idea for children. Again, this area of good practice is populated by uneducated and unqualified "cranks" that with inadequate scientific backgrounds promote daft ideas. The subject of Diabetes has already been raised and this of course is intimately linked to Insulin as well as the consumption of too many highly processed, stomach by-passing meals. The blood Glucose level of mammalian bodies is regulated and strictly maintained at a **constant** figure by the action of hormones, for example, Insulin and Glucagon. This is admittedly a simplistic view but is adequate for our needs. **There is absolutely no scientific reason for continuously feeding to "keep up glucose levels".** This is another one of those daft ideas peddled by "quacks" which encourages people to consume food in the form of snacks at frequent intervals during the day. The easiest way to lose control and consume too many Calories is to "snack" in between set meals. As can be readily imagined, especially in view of previous facts, in general there is a limit to how much food/Calories can be consumed in one sitting. Snacking results in a diet high in Calories and poor in nutrients and has no effect on blood glucose levels!

There is unfortunately, what can only be viewed as, a despicable habit which is prevalent in the majority of schools in the United Kingdom. This is the mid-morning and mid-afternoon break. At a few enlightened schools the only thing allowed to be consumed is water. **Children do not need anything else.** The idea that children should be allowed and even encouraged to consume food at these times is badly flawed!

Some of these schools think they are doing the correct thing because they are following mis-guided government guidelines and encouraging the consumption of fruit, **in between meals.** Whilst this may look like good practice when viewed against the general inadequate fruit eating that takes place, the fruit is full of Calories! (There has also been criticism of the poor fruit quality, another story) The consumption of fruit following a meal should of course be encouraged, for example at lunch time. There is another, even poorer, habit that is now common in schools which is related to the gathering of funding and that is vending machines. Almost inevitably these vending machines are full of high Calorie merchandise, which are consumed both at meal times and between meals. Nutrient value invariably low. Unfortunately, the income derived from these vending machines over-rides the deleterious effect on the health of children.

It is important to restrict food consumption to 3 times per day and there are many secondary social good effects from this habit. It is important to make some attempt at breakfast, a piece of fruit? , and it should be mandatory to stop work and sit down and consume lunch during a proper break. From a business point of view this should be considered good practice, as it will maintain morale, productivity and good health among workers. **It is bad practice to eat lunch over 10 minutes whilst on the move.** Look at the Mediterranean countries way of doing things. Admittedly we lack the temperatures and sunshine but a correct lunch break is essential. An evening family meal should then be viewed as an important social time and not a self-service cafeteria type arrangement. It should take preference over the television etc. Again reflect on comparison with the 1950's when Calorie intake was higher in smaller individuals but both nutrition and fitness were on a higher plane. Family meals were the norm.

GOOD DIET. BALANCE AND MODERATION

Having rubbished a lot of the poor advice, marketing ploys and the dieting industry in general, an indication of good diet is called for. Firstly and most importantly the primary principle **"BALANCE AND MODERATION"**. No food is necessarily bad food, even "fast food" but, it should be consumed in moderation and not as a regular part of routine diet. The most important nutritional piece of information is the Calorie content but for heavens sake don't let this become a domineering item. It should only be used as a guide whilst learning good habits. One thing that has become apparent is food labels are deliberately not made 100% clear. Many labels have energy units written as kcals, this simply means Calories, and watch out for mega-joules.

So what is a good balanced meal? At this point you are maybe beginning to think that half the contents of a so-called "health food shop" are going to be presented or you are going to be advised that a "Nut roast with boiled lettuce" is the answer. Neither is the case. The following may well be something of a surprise but this is "health food" and a good dietary meal;

    Roast Beef
    Yorkshire Pudding
    Potatoes
    Brussels Sprouts
    Carrots
    Cabbage
    All accompanied with 3 glasses of red wine.

How many cranks, quacks and gurus have criticized this type of meal? You cannot possibly eat Roast Beef because Red meat and fat are not good for you. What a load of uneducated nonsense! Remember; Balance **and moderation.** It would not be good for you, as is often the case, to add extra fat when cooking your Rib of Beef but as long as some form of enclosed roasting tin is used, so called self-basting, you cannot go far wrong. The result is a succulent and tender piece of meat with a lot of the natural fat cooked through and out of the joint. This meat is then consumed in moderation and not in vast quantities. The following is an energy breakdown for this meal.

For those older readers 30 grams = 1 ounce

Meat	120grams	300Calories	
Potato	360grams	400Calories	
Brussels Sprouts	120grams	20Calories	
Carrots	120grams	20Calories	
Cabbage	120grams	20Calories	
Yorkshire Pudding	60grams	140Calories	
	900grams	900Calories	(Totals)

This meal, which is supposed to be bad for you, works out at 1 Calorie per gram. The three glasses of red wine add another 300 Calories. The figures are not absolutely precise but this is not important. A general feel for the sort of Calories consumed is enough. Let us know look at a few inferior products that people are buying.

			Cals/gram
Frozen Pizza	400grams	1000Calories	2.5
Frozen whole meal	350grams	400Calories	1.14
Frozen Beef Stew	300grams	300Calories	1
Frozen Lasagne	350grams	400Calories	1.14
Frozen Beef Curry/Rice	400grams	550Calories	1.38
Frozen Beef burgers	320grams	600Calories	1.88
Weight Watchers Frozen;			Cals/gram
Hot Pot	320grams	270Calories	0.84
Chicken Curry	320grams	390Calories	1.22
Shepherds Pie	320grams	240Calories	0.75
Microwave Cheese burger	190grams	600Calories	3.16

One thing is immediately obvious from the list of frozen ready meals; the servings are not very big. In all probability it would be necessary for most people to consume something else to supplement these meals and that is not likely to be a plate of low calorie vegetables. It is quite apparent from the figures for Calories per gram that the so-called unhealthy, traditional meal does very well in comparison to some alternatives. Certainly, it does very well compared to the standard Mcdonalds meal!

The traditional starches are a very important part of a good balanced diet. Again, for some daft reason they get frowned upon when in fact a diet high in bread, rice or potatoes, with fat in moderation, is good for you. The traditional starches provide energy requirements in the correct proportions whilst adding bulk to the diet and hence reduce the need to fill up on other foodstuffs, which may not be so good for you. ie some confectionary high in sugar providing high levels of "empty" Calories. As has already been mentioned the correct diet does not need to contain more than 10% Protein with the remaining energy needs coming from traditional Carbohydrate and Fat. Bulky, traditional starches are what are needed. It cannot be emphasized enough that the modern diet of younger members of society whose Calorie needs have reduced due to a sedentary lifestyle is poor. There is too much non-filling, high-energy food and drinks. Whilst these foodstuffs are all right for a once a week treat they are totally unsuitable for a routine, regular diet. There is also evidence that these diets may well lead to deficiencies of essential vitamins and minerals.

What the "healthy" diet being advocated here shows is how wide of the mark and fraudulent the dieting industry has become. There has obviously developed a need for some members of society to lose weight **FOR HEALTH REASONS** but this has been carried out in a highly unscientific and poorly advised manner. Again it has to be stressed that the only way to correctly lose weight is to match Calorie intake to needs **WHILST** changing lifestyle. This is a simple procedure without the need for dieting clubs, meals or magazines and books advocated by unqualified, uneducated so-called experts. It does not take a vast amount of skill to prepare the meal advocated in this section. The meat cooks itself in an oven and the vegetables only need lightly boiling. The only aspect presenting slight difficulty for the beginner might be the Yorkshire Pudding. Preparing vegetables is simple enough requiring just a little time, which as has already been mentioned society possesses plenty of. There is no need to purchase inedible, unpalatable frozen or chilled ready meals with added sugar, salt and fat together with many other unnatural additives such as preservatives and antioxidants. We are doing our children and future generations a disservice by failing to pass on good dietary practices and the **simple** ability to prepare and cook sound, healthy meals. Much of this would develop by going back to families sitting down and eating together, meals like the one advocated. If children are brought up eating vegetables they will continue to do so the rest of their life and eating together should include preparing food together.

OTHER NUTRIENTS.

As well as the three main food groups, Carbohydrate, Fat and Protein it is important that other essential nutrients are consumed for use in the metabolism of organisms. These minor nutrients are obtained from a whole range of food types and are another reason for having a balanced diet. One thing research has shown is that these minor nutrients do not work so well if they are taken as extracted supplements compared with obtaining them from whole food. Yet another reason for making it a habit to consume a balanced diet. That is not to say there is no place for supplements and herbal remedies. Many of these can form valuable functions in daily life bearing in mind the principle of balance and moderation. Many plants contain chemicals, which may be of benefit to us from a medical point of view.

It is essential for most of life that we have a supply of Oxygen and Sunlight, so one would assume that these two items could not be harmful which is unfortunately not the case. Oxygen is a highly reactive element involved in the production of many chemical compounds. Everyone knows the effect of Oxygen on Iron with the resultant corrosion known as rust. Within living organisms, this element that we continuously breath in, is responsible for the formation of a number of harmful compounds such as, hydroxide ions (-OH), peroxide (H_2O_2) and something called "free radicals". The body needs to counteract these harmful chemicals and it does this by using something called "anti-oxidants" obtained from the diet. In the plant world, the energy from sunlight, which is used to power photosynthesis, naturally also generates harmful Oxygen compounds and free radicals. Plants counteract this by producing the same anti-oxidants that we then use to protect ourselves. One of the most important anti-oxidants is Vitamin C, which is found in much plant material, especially some fruit. This is one reason for the drive to encourage more fruit eating in school children.

The disease called "Cancer" can be thought to occur when the DNA of cells is damaged by harmful chemicals, which are either consumed or produced within the body. It is also thought that the multi-factorial disease called Coronary Heart Disease is helped by the consumption of fruit and vegetables and it is partly to prevent these two diseases that it is advocated that 5 portions of fruit and vegetables are consumed daily. The following is by no means a comprehensive list but it will give a rough idea of the advantages of having a varied diet consumed with Balance and Moderation.

Vitamin A
A fat soluble Vitamin found in Fish, Liver and dairy products whilst its precursor is found in fruit and vegetables. ie "carotene". It is needed for vision and for protein synthesis and DNA repair.

Vitamin B1 (Thiamine)
A water-soluble vitamin found in small amounts in many grains. It is a co-enzyme used in the conversion of Glucose to energy. Deficiency causes the disease called "Beri-beri". There is a hint these days that a deficiency is being seen in those consuming an "empty calorie diet"

Vitamin B2 (Riboflavin)
Water-soluble found in dairy products. It is a coenzyme used in energy production and for the repair of tissues.

Vitamin B6 (Pyridoxine)
A water-soluble vitamin found in many sources. Pyridoxine is necessary for good nerve and brain function.

Vitamin B12
A water-soluble vitamin found in meat, fish and dairy products. It is needed for DNA synthesis and for healthy nerves. Deficiency is related to Pernicious Anaemia.

Folic Acid
Water-soluble found in grains and leafy vegetables. It is needed for DNA and RNA metabolism and plays a vital role in pregnancy.

Vitamin C (Ascorbic Acid)
A water-soluble vitamin found in fruit and brassicas. It is needed for the production of collagen, for iron absorption and is a powerful anti-oxidant. Collagen is the basis of connective tissue and therefore is vital for healthy blood vessels, bones, muscles and gums. Deficiency causes Scurvy, characterized by poor gums and loss of teeth, and iron deficiency anaemia.

Vitamin D

A fat-soluble vitamin found in fish and dairy products. The body produces it internally by the reaction of sunlight on the skin. Deficiency causes softening of bone tissue and the related diseases Rickets and Osteomalacia. It is being seen again due to the sedentary, indoor lifestyle being adopted.

Vitamin E

A fat-soluble vitamin found in dietary oils. It is an important anti-oxidant and needed for healthy blood vessels.

Vitamin K

A fat-soluble vitamin found in Liver and Brassicas. It is vital for blood clotting.

Calcium

Found in Dairy products and fish. It is related to Vitamin D levels. Needed for Bones, nerve impulses, and muscle contraction and for communication within cells.

Iron

Found in a variety of sources. Needed for Haemoglobin and electron transport.

Selenium

Found in meat and fish and those vegetables grown in Selenium rich soils. Needed as an anti-oxidant.

Zinc

Found in fish, meat and grains. It is needed for growth.

As an example of the beneficial effects of plant material it is useful to look at that group of plants called Brassicas. This group of plants is full of "Phytochemicals" which are responsible for much of their smell and taste. Unfortunately, this wonderful group of food plants is not eaten by much of the population, which is a great pity. This may be another good reason for family meals and the education of the younger generations to enjoy these good foods. The Phytochemicals are known to protect against certain cancers. In Brussels sprouts there is a chemical called "Sinigrin" which has a very powerful effect against cancer cells and in fact causes death of the malignant cells. This effect has been found at relatively low levels of Sinigrin and it is therefore advocated that a small helping of Brussels sprouts at weekly intervals can have a very beneficial effect. Broccoli has a chemical called "Sulphoraphane" which although does not kill cancer cells it blocks their continued development and therefore is yet again very beneficial. It has been shown that the mix of these Phytochemicals from "whole" foods is far more useful than taking the extracted chemicals as supplements. Returning to the question of red meat, the protective effect of fruit and vegetables is enough to nullify the adverse effect of the meat. Yet again we come back to the sensible practice of Balance and Moderation. There is no harm in eating Meat and Dairy products as long as they are balanced by Fruit and Vegetables and consumed in moderation. The health scares and silly diets promoted by unqualified and uneducated quacks and cranks should be consigned to the dustbin where they belong. Humans are omnivores who will do very well on a **Moderate and Balanced** diet, as many of the population will demonstrate. We are failing some of the younger generations with our lamentably poor eating and social habits.

APPLES

Earlier on in this book the supermarkets in Britain have been abused regarding their retail and marketing practices. This is well illustrated by the shocking account of the sale of apples in our supermarkets. This country has a history of over 4000 different varieties of Apple and as was explained many of them were suited to quite small and specific localities. Things have changed and in Britain the most common variety of apple now grown and sold is Cox's Orange Pippin. This is somewhat different to the picture in the rest of the world where the four most common varieties are; Golden Delicious, Delicious, Gala and the new variety Fuji. The biggest, by far, Apple producer in the world now is China and 50% of their apples are the variety "Fuji". With this country's tradition for apple growing you would think that our supermarkets would have a range of virtually all-British apples. Unfortunately this is not the case.

The apple selling market in this country is worth well over £300 Million and the supermarkets are responsible for 70% of these sales. Unfortunately, the proportion of British apples sold by the supermarkets only accounts for about 35% of total sales. Even in the height of the British apple season the supermarkets don't tend to do better than about 50% British Apples. The supermarkets also lay down very strict criteria for the apples sold which leads to an increase in Pesticide sprays applied to the fruit. In the recent past the supermarkets have rejected Apples for the following reasons;

Minor Blemishes
Apples too Red
Apples not Red enough
Apples too big
Apples too small
Apples the wrong shape

The only thing Apples are not rejected for is their nutritional content, which is apparently unimportant. An Apple is about 10% Carbohydrate (a mix of sugars), 4% Vitamins and about 80% water. Supermarkets import Cox's Apples from New Zealand, a distance of 14,000 miles, whilst British Cox's Apples lie rotting on the ground because there are no buyers. There are any number of reports, which show that stored fruit and vegetables that are transported huge distances lose their nutritional value. This means that the Vitamin C content of the imported New Zealand Apples is dramatically reduced. **Where**

is the sense in that? Apples can play a big part in the 5 portions of fruit and vegetables per day, BUT NOT USING THE SUPERMARKETS CRITERIA!

The world has gone mad. Here are some figures for food imports/exports for 1998.

	Imported	Exported
Bread	174,570 tons	148,710 tons
Eggs	21,979 tons	30,604 tons
Pork	158,294 tons	258,558 tons

The figures for that most British of Fruit growing probably make horrendous reading with imports at a totally ridiculous level. How much are the supermarkets to blame for the dietary ill health being exhibited by a large proportion of the nation? It is already acknowledged that their economic costs to the traditional food producers of this country together with the hidden environmental costs of transport and pesticide use are enormous.

Chapter 7

POLLUTION

It may seem strange to continue with this as a subject but as will be seen it is in fact a natural next step. It must be stressed immediately that the following is NO criticism of individual farmers or Medical practitioners. The farming community in the United Kingdom has been badly led and advised over many years with the result that it has been dictated to by the large Agri-chemical companies and the large Supermarket chains. The effect of this has been a disaster for the environment, health and wealth problems for the individual farmers and an increase in unnatural and unpleasant chemical residues in foodstuffs affecting the whole population. Farmers have been encouraged by their so-called leaders to carry out unnatural practices in their daily lives with terrible consequences. Farmers were continually assured that what they were doing was correct and if one chemical was not effective there was always another one waiting to be let loose into the environment. Not surprisingly, many farmers lost sight of what had been a sustainable way of life, by carrying out the recommendations of the governments of the day. Unfortunately, successive governments had a blinkered and unnatural idea about the growing and breeding of foodstuffs. Always the same when politicians get involved in matters they have no tradition, background or understanding of. The result is we now have a developed world where foodstuffs are routinely contaminated with artificial, synthetic chemicals at a falsely depressed cost to the consumer and the farming community in tatters with severely lowered numbers. The average age of farmers is in the fifties because very few people are entering to take their place. How long will cheap, polluted imports stay cheap when we are unable to produce them ourselves?

Let us make one thing very clear so there can be no confusion;
NO level of synthetic chemical is safe.
There is NO safe limit of synthetic chemical.

The levels given in various publications for safe dosages/ limits of chemicals in food/drink/the environment are **arbitrary. They have never been proven.** These limits have been determined by extrapolation from other species experiments which may be short term and not relevant to the circumstances in humans. There is little or no effort to determine what effect a mixture or cocktail of chemicals may have. It is all very well to conduct tests on one chemical in isolation but we humans are continually exposed to dozens of chemicals with no idea what effect the mixture may have. There is also the problem of accumulation. It is a well known ecological fact that as food passes up the food chain, for example to humans, chemicals will be concentrated. Some of the synthetic chemicals, which have been produced by mankind, are naturally fat-soluble and therefore have been stored within fat tissues of species. Which organ has a big percentage of fat and a huge blood supply? **The Brain.** The fat is naturally present as insulation for nerve fibres, making nerve impulses more efficient. Therefore, although the daily intake of a chemical may be much less than the arbitrary daily limit, it could accumulate over time. It really is no surprise that arbitrary limits fall over time as more becomes known of chemical effects and also that many chemicals get banned as time goes by. Whether a chemical is banned can depend on the individual country and its responsible behaviour to the health of its citizens.

Let us return to earlier in the book and the subjects of biochemistry and genetics. It was shown that DNA was simply a code for the production of proteins and that many of these proteins were present to act as Enzymes for the many chemical reactions that take place in living organisms. One of the important processes was called Catabolism, which was the breakdown of organic molecules, by many Enzymes into CO_2, H_2O, Urea and energy. It obviously required the correct "Genes" to be present for this to take place. As a simple example let us look at Vitamin C. Vitamin C is made from Glucose by a small number of chemical reactions controlled by about half a dozen Enzymes. The vast majority of living organisms have the genes to produce these Enzymes and so can produce their own Vitamin C. Humans DNA has the gene missing for the last Enzyme in the process and therefore cannot make their own Vitamin C, with the result that it needs to be taken in daily. A very important point can therefore be made. We either must have the Enzymes (and hence genes) present to breakdown chemicals taken in OR we must have a means of excreting them intact with no adverse effects.

Therefore, any chemicals we take in should ideally be derived from an organic source of a material we would naturally use, i.e. a normal food product. If we take in a chemical, which our bodies are not designed to digest, and breakdown completely then we could harm ourselves. If we have not got the genes and Enzymes necessary for the complete breakdown of a chemical then harmful residues could be retained. If the chemicals or their residues are fat soluble then they may be retained in fat tissues and stores. They could therefore accumulate and of course chemicals stored around nerve tissue may interfere with nerve impulses. All of this has most certainly happened in the past and although some lessons have been learned there is still a ready acceptance of far too many chemicals and also a massive business in the production of new ones.

Sources of Pollution are;
>Food Additives
>Agriculture and Horticulture
>Medicine
>Industry
>Vaccines (Armed Forces)

FOOD ADDITIVES

There are a ridiculously high number of Additives in modern processed food. Indeed, in some processed products the word food is probably totally inappropriate to describe it. Whilst most people's idea of food additives might be small quantities of strange chemicals, processed food is renowned for having large amounts of SALT, SUGAR and FAT added. It is the only way to make them remotely palatable. It has been shown frequently in opinion polls that the general public think food additives are bad and unnecessary, but they are still increasing.

At the end of the Second World War there were less than 1000 processed foods available in the United Kingdom. At present there are now over 10,000 different food products available in the United Kingdom.

The Additives that are added to food products can be roughly divided into two broad categories. There are the Preservatives and Antioxidants, which are put in to increase the shelf life and stop the product deteriorating. The other group is a multi-functional collection which are designed to make the product more attractive. The preservatives and antioxidants were often an excuse for bad practices, which then needed other additives such as colourings to mask their effect. Even those additives made from "natural" products have not turned out to be safe. Some of these "natural" products were from plant sources, which Mankind never consumed. Also, some of these "natural" products were in fact synthetically manufactured. This can be demonstrated by the use of Beetroot dye for colouring. This is harmless to us when consumed in beetroot, retained within beetroot cells. When this dye used either in an extracted state or synthetically produced it can be harmful to parts of the alimentary tract.

Everyone has become aware of "E- numbers" listed on the packaging of food products. These are in fact very misleading and many are totally harmless. Even Carbon dioxide, Oxygen and Hydrogen have "E-numbers" for instance! The problem is how to determine those, which are potentially harmful from the many harmless. Another problem, which quite frankly is a deceit, is that Flavourings are not listed by name. There are over 3,500 flavourings, which are allowed to be added to food products. The result is that those novelty foods and snacks, such as sauces, soups, savouries and desserts, can be made to taste of ANYTHING. In fact the basic ingredients of all of these products can be the same but the use of colour, texture and flavour additives produce what appears to be different products. What is most certainly true of all of them is that the final product is VERY POOR NUTRITIONALLY.

Many of the food additives have been shown to cause problems in some individuals. They are known to cause Allergies with resultant Rashes, Dermatitis, Eczema, Headaches and Asthma. They also are known to cause intolerance reactions leading to hyperactivity and behavioural problems. There is also the problem of additive "Cocktails" which have never been adequately tested.

There are over 300 "E-numbers" and the list below is the broad categories they are divided into.

"E"		
	100-180	Colours
	200-285	Preservatives
	300-321	Antioxidants
	322-495	Emulsifiers / Stabilizers
	500-578	Processing Aids
	620-637	Flavour Enhancers
	920-927	Bleaches
	953-959	Sweeteners
	1200-1520	Modified Starches

The group of chemicals from number 322 to number 1520 have the following range of functions.

Acids, acidity regulators, anti-caking agents, anti-foaming agents, bulking agents, carriers and carrier solvents, emulsifiers, firming agents, flavour enhancers, foaming agents, glazing agents, humectants, modified starches, packaging gases, propellants, raising agents, sequestrants, sweeteners, bleaches. As an example of the "madness" of "E-numbers" let us look at two related chemicals, which should **NEVER** have been used in food products; E 320 and E 321.

The starting point for these two E-numbers is a molecule called BENZENE. You may have heard of this chemical, as it is a constituent of PETROL. It is also used in Dry - Cleaning and as a general Fat solvent. We need to introduce a little chemistry again to explain what the idiots in the food industry are doing. The chemical formula for BENZENE is C_6H_6 and is thought of as a ring structure. If you replace one of the Hydrogen atoms with a Methyl group - - - CH_3 then we get C_7H_8 which is a chemical called TOLUENE. If you then add an Oxygen atom to Toluene you get C_7H_8O, which is a chemical called ANISOLE. Let us now give the proper names to the E-numbers 320 and 321.

E 320   Butylated Hydroxy ANISOLE
E 321   Butylated Hydroxy TOLUENE

These two chemicals are some of the most commonly used antioxidants in processed food. They are commonly used where there are Fats or Oils in food products (presumably to prevent rancidity) and are hence found in biscuits, confectionery, and crisps, processed meats and often in packet mixes for sauces and desserts. Not surprisingly in view of their background these two chemicals are linked to serious health problems. They are both known to cause rashes and skin irritation, hyperactivity, liver damage, mutagenic to DNA and Cancer.

Which "BARMPOT" dreamt up the idea of putting Benzene derivatives in food?

Would you pour Petrol over your breakfast cereal? Would you marinate your meat in it to preserve it? And yet the food manufacturers are happily doing just that with these highly toxic chemicals. Living Organisms were never designed to come into contact with these sorts of chemicals and yet in the name of Profit the food manufacturers happily mix them with food products of very suspect nutritional value.

In the United Kingdom, food additives are considered safe and tested. In view of the above two chemicals "YOU DECIDE".

There is a different view taken in other parts of the world where food additives allowed in the United Kingdom are either banned or restricted.

The labelling of Food Additives is suspect and filled with loopholes. 3,500 flavouring agents, which do not have to be listed. The processed food industry and their products cannot be good for us and it is surely not a good idea to consume and rely on them on a daily basis.

PESTICIDES

The word "Pesticide" needs to be explained a little. People in general would view the word "pest" as meaning perhaps an insect such as an Aphid but this does not mean that pesticides are simply insecticides. The word "Pesticide" is a broad term covering a wide range of "killing" agents, which mostly relate to plants. A Pesticide covers Insecticides, Herbicides, and Fungicides and also can be applied to chemicals, which kill Mites, Molluscs, Worms and Rodents. By their very nature Pesticides are designed to "Kill" something and therefore they are "Toxic" chemicals. Mankind has not been very intelligent in the use and production of these chemicals. As has been intimated throughout this book the over-riding principle has been "economic" and not safety. The large Corporations that have been responsible for the development of these chemicals have failed to take into account the Biochemistry, Genetics and Metabolism of living organisms with the result that our environment has been poisoned and continues to be poisoned. For economic reasons, Agriculture is no longer about growing necessary crops in harmony with the rest of nature and the environment. Instead our poor farmers have been conditioned into a manufacturing process requiring HUGE and expensive chemical inputs often to produce dubious crops. The crop called "RAPE" is aptly named for what it is doing to our countryside and it must be the worst "blot on the landscape" mankind has ever invented. This unsightly crop causes misery to many with its pollen and requires unacceptable amounts of toxic chemicals at vast expense. The small number of large Corporations, producing the chemicals (including artificial fertilizers) and seed, has become very powerful and rich on this unhealthy practice. The result has been a large reduction in the number people working on the land, with the large input costs helping to make it unprofitable. The average age of farmers in the United Kingdom is well above 50, with little incentive for younger people to carry on the tradition. The land is polluted, wildlife has suffered and with the vicious circle "treadmill" that small farmers find themselves in it is not surprising that farming is in crisis.

How long will cheap food imports stay cheap after we lose the workforce to produce our own food?

As an example of the hidden costs associated with modern agriculture ponder the following "accepted" fact. The cost, in the United Kingdom, of cleaning up water that has been polluted by agricultural practices amounts to over £120 **Million per year.** That is what it costs to make water fit again for human consumption.

In January 2003, a study was carried out in the United States of America into the concentrations of Pesticides found in children. It was shown that children eating a "conventional" diet had pesticide concentrations 6 times higher than those children who had eaten an "organic" diet. This difference was due to the pesticide residues found in normal conventional food. THE HUMAN BODY WAS NOT DESIGNED TO DEAL WITH ANY OF THESE UNNATURAL CHEMICALS. How can anybody think they are safe in ANY concentration? There is NO evidence to show the safety of these chemicals within humans. They are made to be TOXIC. The figures given for safe levels are arbitrary guesses derived no doubt from extrapolated animal experiments funded by the large Corporations with a vested interest.

The chemicals now used in "developed" nations have gone through an evolutionary process, which meant the early chemicals were banned, as their side effects became known. The process of banning chemicals continues and a large number were dropped in the year 2003, although many of these were for economic reasons as the more rigorous testing procedures being introduced made them unviable. The following is an illustration of the history of Pesticides.

One of the early groups of pesticides was the Organochlorides. A common example of this is the well-known **D.D.T.** These chemicals were very toxic and effective at controlling insect pests. They had a very severe drawback. The organochlorides do not breakdown, degrade or undergo catabolism very readily and their half-life can be measured in decades. The result is that they persist in the environment and can still be found in sediments from agricultural "run-off". They also therefore Bioaccumulate in living organisms. What this means is that organochlorides, because they don't degrade, are stored within living organisms, often in fat tissue. When these organisms are then in turn consumed the organchloride within them is stored within the consumer, again possibly within fat stores. The problem, which then occurs of course, is that consuming organisms consume many polluted organisms and therefore the concentration of the organochloride continues to rise with tragic consequences. The large pesticide manufacturing Corporations initially refused to accept what was going on with the result that huge numbers of wildlife were destroyed, especially birds. Mankind of course was also consuming and storing large amounts of organochlorides. **D.D.T** was banned in the U.S.A. in 1972 but it is still found in the environment and in food there today. This is due to two factors. One is its persistence so it is still found in water and earth and it travels in water and wind. The other factor is it is found in imported food from "developing" countries who incredibly are still using it. There are serious health effects and it is implicated in Cancer, Neurological Damage and Birth defects.

One point that needs to be made. One of the biggest stores of Fat in the human body is the Brain. Therefore, any fat-soluble chemical taken in can accumulate in the Brain. If that chemical is then not readily broken down and persists it is a comforting thought. It is no surprise that Neurological problems are associated with environmental pollutants.

In March 2001, a report was released in the U.S.A. called "Nowhere to Hide". This was a report into Persistent Organic Pollutants, toxic chemicals, within the U.S.A. food supply. It found that;

"Virtually all food products are contaminated with Persistent Organic Pollutants"

These Persistent Organic Pollutants (P.O.P.) are derived from four main sources;

1. Pesticides
2. Industrial Chemicals
3. By-Products of manufacturing Processes
4. Waste Incineration

The organochloride pesticides have been largely superseded by a group of insecticides called Organophospates. These chemicals do not persist in the environment but they are common and used in vast quantities. They are known to affect the nervous system and are endocrine disrupters, which affect the sex hormones. In 2003, research showed that there was a positive link between the use of these chemicals and "Chronic Fatigue Syndrome".

Another "infamous" pesticide is the Herbicide "Atrazine". This chemical persists in ground water and hence leaches into watercourses and ponds. There is evidence that it may cause Prostate cancer in humans. What has now been firmly established is that in incredibly small doses, Atrazine causes sex reversal in Male Frogs with calamitous effects on the Frog population numbers. Atrazine has recently been banned in the United Kingdom, although typically loopholes have been left allowing some use. The U.S.A. still uses this unpleasant chemical in large quantities, especially in the growing of Maize.

As has been mentioned previously, Pesticides tend to be tested on animals individually and there is little attempt to find out what effect may occur when they are mixed up. It has already been mentioned that the food supply seems to be contaminated with many different pesticide residues and no one knows what effect this cocktail could be having. There are four possible effects;

1. Simple additive effect.
2. Two chemicals have completely separate effects.
3. Synergy. An enhanced effect.
4. Antagonism . A reduced effect. A higher dose needs to be given.

Who is to know what effects, over a long period of time, could be occurring???

In the United Kingdom, in 1997, the government, via the Food Standards Agency, gave the following advice;

"All fruit and vegetables should be peeled before consumption, because of the risk posed from pesticide residues".

For political reasons an attempt was made to change this advice, when there was no change in the number of pesticide residues and no change in safety factors. At the moment it is advocated, quite rightly, that people should consume 5 portions of fruit and vegetables a day. But, at maximum residue levels this is completely unsafe for children. Endocrine disrupter pesticide residues are commonly found on fruit and young children are VERY vulnerable to these endocrine disrupters as their reproductive systems are actively developing at this stage. The government are also expanding and developing their scheme of free fruit to children of a certain age to be distributed at primary school. The advice is that this free fruit, given at the wrong time (between meals), should be peeled before being consumed. How safe is this fruit with advice like that? Is this a flawed idea to make up for the selling off of school playing fields?

Is this nothing but a bad taste political statement?

To sum up Pesticides here is a list of their drawbacks;

1. Human Poisoning
2. Environmental Hazards
3. Insufficient Testing and long term side effects. Human Metabolism.
4. Loss of Biodiversity
5. Wildlife Deaths
6. Interference with natural Pest control
7. Develops resistance among Pests
8. Residues in food
9. Water Pollution
10. They are Expensive Inputs

This last point is very important Globally, especially in the developing world. Traditional crop varieties give lower yields but less pests and low inputs. Large Corporations have foisted new varieties giving bigger yields **BUT** more pests, high inputs, poorer storage and eventually therefore, similar yield at greater cost. The end result is **MORE DEBT.**

FISH FARMING

An accepted problem at the moment is the depletion of fish stocks and the need to conserve and ration fishing of some species. To this end, a small number of entrepreneurial crofters in Scotland set up fish farms. These initial small concerns produced a SMALL number of fish in good, acceptable and healthy conditions. Unfortunately, rather like the unacceptable and disgusting conditions that much of our poultry and eggs are bred in, the fish farm concerns attracted business people with no idea about animal welfare. Having made a success out of clean and healthy, low-density fish farming, other people saw an opportunity to make a large profit with no regard for the final product. If "X" number of fish in a tank made "Y" number of pounds profit then "10X" number of fish in the same tank would make at least "10Y" profit. The result stinks, and really nobody should have been surprised at the recent public announcement concerning the safety of the fish from these outrageously dirty environments. The factory farming fish producers, who have formed a powerful restricted club, of course cried "foul" over their unworthy products. They would have us believe that their products are good and wholesome and yet if the truth is known they are bred in disgusting and totally unnatural conditions and the final offering is packed full of pesticide residues. Heaven help the poor COD if these unscrupulous people succeed in their plans to exploit this fish.

Understandably, the United Kingdom now consumes a lot of a crustacean known as Prawns or Shrimps. It is generally thought that these fish are caught out at sea but in fact at least a third of the Prawns or Shrimps consumed in "developed" nations come from farms. The major sources are the U.S.A. and Asia. Whereas the U.S.A. has some control over the chemical inputs into these operations unfortunately the Asian source are less careful. The Prawns or Shrimps are cultured in large artificial ponds, which are managed in a purely commercial manner. There is a high use of Pesticides used and they are of four groups; Organochlorides, Organophosphates, Carbamates and then a variety of others. Many of these chemicals are classified from extremely hazardous to simply hazardous to human health and would not be allowed in "developed" nations. There are also of course pollution problems to the local community with these operations. Thus;

1. The effluent from the "culture ponds" enters watercourses, which are used eventually for drinking water.

2. Those people applying the chemicals suffer from poisoning.

3. There is poisoning and skin disease from the water pollution.

4. There is the obvious accumulation of Pesticides into the Prawn/Shrimp and the resultant residues movement up the food chain.

There is also a large input of Artificial Fertilizers, Disinfectants, Feed Additives, Steroids, Probiotics, Vitamins, Immuno-stimulants, and Antibiotics.

In the 1960's Fish farms were started in Scottish inland waters and seas. By the 1980's this had developed into a thriving cottage industry giving work to a small number of crofters and producing a good product, which was raised sympathetically in low numbers. ie Farmed Salmon. By the year 2000 this cottage industry had grown by about 160 times and three-quarters of it was controlled by large multi-national companies. These fish farms were bigger and run on a far more intensive level. The fish have the equivalent of half a human bathtub to swim in and the sheltered conditions used mean they swim around in their own excrement. These intensive conditions mean that parasite levels are enormous and disease is rife. The salmon is normally a "Top predator" fish living off other fish and crustaceans. Farmed salmon lives off feed, which is ground up grain, poultry by-products and small fish. It takes 3 pounds of caught small fish to produce 1 pound of salmon, which of course does nothing for the conservation of some fish stocks. This ground up feed is high in fat, which does not suit the salmon and leads to diarrhoea. The salmon sometimes escape from the cages they are bred in and they have been shown to mate and hybridize with wild salmon and trout and pass on diseases and parasites. Wild salmon numbers have declined dramatically in those rivers, which have salmon farms related to them. The fish farms act as sources of "raw sewage" which discharge into these rivers, which leads to unnatural algal growth and the release of toxins.

The salmon in these caged fish farms do not get a natural diet and therefore they are grey in colour. To make the salmon pink, which is expected by consumers, a synthetic colour additive is put into the water called CANTHAXANTHIN. This material is banned as a food additive but apparently it is all right to give it to the salmon, which we then eat! To counteract the parasitic Sea-lice a large quantity of chemicals such as CYPERMETHRIN is added to the water. This is a toxic material, which is also an Endocrine disrupter. Many other chemicals have been used such as organochlorides, other insecticides and antibiotics. Because salmon are oily fish, then as was explained previously, fat-soluble toxic chemicals will tend to accumulate and even wild fish are found with residues from the environment. Before the salmon can be "harvested" they need to be purged and so for the last 30 days they are removed from the cages and they are not fed for the final 10 days of their lives.

MEDICINE

As was mentioned earlier there is no criticism of the medical profession implied here and it is **NOT advocated that prescribed drugs from your doctor are not taken.** We need to reiterate a statement made earlier, there is no safe level of a synthetic chemical, although in general that does not mean a synthetic copy of a naturally occurring chemical. The medical profession are mostly only concerned with one thing and that is treating and looking after their patients. They prescribe drugs in the manner they were taught to try to make their patients better. They strongly believe in the beneficial properties of these drugs and in general are so busy and hard working that perhaps they cannot see a wider picture as their "noses are pressed hard against the glass". It is also accepted by the medical profession that their training and emphasis is based on curing people and not the prevention of disease. Consequently, the medical profession are probably not the best people to ask for advice regarding things like diet. This is creating difficulties in the fight against things like Obesity, Calorie control and lack of exercise.

Returning to synthetic chemicals, as has been stated and will stand repeating, due reference to biochemistry needs to be kept in mind .The satisfactory metabolism and excretion of end products is important and with this in mind, drugs that are derived from organic plant based sources may be kinder than purely synthetic chemicals made artificially in the laboratory. It is not surprising that the large companies which are responsible for synthetic Agri-chemicals, industrial pollution and food additives are the same companies producing many of the drugs used by the medical profession. Yet again the over-riding factor in much of drug production is the making of greater profits and not better safer drugs. A recent headline from one of these major drug companies suggested that many of their products did not work very efficiently and in some people not at all! That is a comforting thought when someone, at often-great expense, takes a potent synthetic chemical and swallows it!

Many modern drugs, quite naturally in view of their mode of action, are also prone to quite serious side effects with the result that further drugs need to be taken to counter-act this phenomenon. Perhaps more effort should be given to cheaper kinder alternatives although this is unlikely due to the lower profits generated. A recent article in The LANCET highlights this and states that modern expensive drugs are often not as effective as cheaper old-fashioned remedies. As an example is the Diuretic CHLOTHALIDONE which costs only a few pence per pill. This drug appears to be more effective at lowering blood pressure than all the modern alternatives, which are pushed at the medical profession strongly because the profit is greater. This practice is also readily seen with common "over the counter" remedies. One of mankind's most valuable drugs is ASPIRIN, which is extremely cheap when bought simply as Aspirin. Unfortunately, by simply giving it a different name and packaging it differently the general public is duped into paying a vast amount more for this simple and highly effective product.

An area of concern at present is ANTIBIOTICS. These drugs have not been used wisely by mankind and their misuse has led to the severe problem of antibiotic resistance. Again, the large companies have not helped this in a number of ways. For economic reasons there is little research and development into finding more effective antibiotics to overcome the problem of resistance. An absolutely abhorrent habit is still occurring and that is the use of antibiotics as growth promoters in animal feed for domestic animals, which end up in the human food chain. This again is occurring due to the seeking of higher profits by the large Agri-chemical companies. Antibiotics should have been a restricted drug, used sparingly, for essential infective conditions. They should NOT have been widely present in the environment. You would think the lesson of the last 40 years would have been learnt? If we return to the problem of inserting new genetic material into Genetically Modified organisms, one of the techniques is to use Antibiotic Inhibitor Genes. This means that these plants will naturally be resistant to certain antibiotics and this resistance can be passed on to bacteria when the plant is consumed! This really makes sense!!!

As an example of the potential difficulties, which may occur from prescribed drug therapy let us, look at a commonly prescribed drug called AMIODARONE. This drug is used as an Anti-Arrhythmic agent, which makes the heart, beat better. It requires quite a bit of time and effort to get the patient stabilized and the dosage correct but is very effective at correcting problems with the heartbeat. Unfortunately, this drug has considerable problems from a side effect viewpoint and exhibits a lot of the worries highlighted earlier from a biochemistry point of view. The body cannot get rid of Amiodarone very easily as its metabolites are not completely broken down and the body has difficulty in excreting these metabolites. The result is that it can take a long time to remove it from the body after stopping the therapy. Like many of the worries highlighted earlier with synthetic chemicals, what happens if they are fat-soluble? Amiodarone is a chemical whose metabolites are stored in fat tissue, which of course would include the Brain. To get rid of the metabolites they have to be excreted in the bile via the liver. They are not cleared from the bloodstream via the kidneys and urine. The end result is that it can take the body 4 months to get rid of this drug after taking it. The major side effects of taking this drug include; Pulmonary Fibrosis, Corneal deposits, Facial pigmentation, Peripheral Neuropathy, Gastro-Intestinal effects, Central Nervous System effects (hardly surprising with the metabolites stored there) and Liver disfunction. Also, because Amiodarone contains Iodine it tends to disrupt the Thyroid Gland.

This drug **Graphically illustrates** the potential problems when a Synthetic chemical, which the human body was not designed to deal with, finds its way into the human body. Whereas the medical profession are probably fully justified in asking their patients to take potent chemicals in an effort to make them well, **there is not the same justification for the use of synthetic chemicals in Agriculture, Horticulture and especially Food Production.**

It maybe possible to now draw the various strands of Pollution together in raising the doubts which are beginning to exist concerning one of mankind's supposed afflictions, POLIO. The evidence at the moment is perhaps circumstantial and also politically very embarrassing but it is just possible that this disorder is in fact a man-made problem. Polio is in fact a relatively recent phenomenon, which seems to have appeared at the same time as synthetic Agricultural chemicals came into being. There is now a school of thought that the disease called Polio is in fact simply the effects of poisoning by Pesticides. At the moment the areas in the world where Polio is still present are those areas where control and safety of Agricultural chemicals are not what they should be. Consider also two events, which have affected the developed world. Farmers who have used tanks of chemicals to dip sheep in, to control pests on the sheep, have suffered various health problems, which may bear a resemblance to the symptoms of Polio. Secondly, there has been a barely acknowledged problem in armed service personnel who were treated with a range of synthetic chemicals whilst serving in alien and hostile environments. Again, these military personnel have suffered from a range of disorders, which could be likened to the disease known as Polio. It is likely, in future years, that mankind's indiscriminate use of synthetic toxic chemicals will throw up a number of conditions, which are proven to be caused by this dubious practice.

Chapter 8
FINALE

This narrative was an attempt to explain how "LIFE" works in layman's terms based on established scientific principles. Virtually all living organisms use the same biochemical processes to maintain their existence. The importance of the molecule **ATP** has been shown as the unit of currency for the production of energy. The structure and use of the three major substances that we know of as food has been described. The breakdown of food has been shown to be controlled by a vast number of ENZYMES and it has been shown that the mysterious subject of Genetics is actually relatively simple and concerned primarily with the production of these Enzymes. The divisions of energy production have been explained and it was shown that the most important element in our daily energy expenditure was **BASAL METABOLIC RATE.** Basal metabolic rate varies with the size and age of the individual and it is possible to adjust the level so that individuals can raise or lower it depending upon lifestyle. To demonstrate this let us look at a very common event, which is probably the over-riding principle of life, REPRODUCTION.

It is possible to measure Basal Metabolic Rate under controlled conditions and over the years the methods for doing this have become more accurate. There have been a number of studies, both in the developed and in the developing world, into the Basal Metabolic Rate of pregnant females. This is another area of misconception (!) as it was wrongly assumed that a large increase in calorie intake was required. When the figures are looked at closely this proves not to be the case and the widespread idea that "you should eat for two" has proved to be wrong. Comparison between pregnant women in developed countries and developing countries, such as West Africa, has been very revealing. It has been estimated that the minimal extra weight associated with pregnancy is of the order of 8-9 kilograms. This is the weight of the fetal element combined with the necessary maternal changes but not the extra fat, which often is deposited. Pregnancy lasts for about 40 weeks, so the extra weight gain necessary is about 0.2 kilograms per week, or about 0.03 kilograms per day. This is somewhat erroneous as the weight gain is not spread evenly over the pregnancy, but it does not alter the underlying principle. It has been calculated that for this minimal weight gain, the extra energy requirement is of the order of 20,000 Calories, or about 70 Calories per day. This is about a 3% increase in the number of extra Calories needed, which immediately throws into question the need to "eat for two". Women in the developing world, such as West Africa, are quite possibly living on a diet where food is restricted and their working life does not change due to pregnancy. How do they find the extra Calories needed for pregnancy? The answer is both simple and evolutionary advantageous, **THEY LOWER THEIR BASAL METABOLIC RATE.** This phenomenon has been demonstrated in the developed world also, and may have a cultural/racial element. Most of the growth in pregnancy takes place in the final third, and therefore it is only during this period that more Calories are required. Whilst Basal Metabolic Rate tends to rise during the final third of pregnancy, women tend to become less active during this time and so their energy requirements decrease. The end result is that West African females on a restricted diet produce perfectly healthy babies of an acceptable weight. This again has been readily seen in the developed world. It is now accepted that one cannot lay down strict guidelines for weight gain during pregnancy because it is perfectly acceptable for some women to lose weight. This is achieved by **lowering their basal metabolic rate and lowering their core temperature a little.** It is thought that this is a major physiological advantage in women living on a restricted diet.

This is more powerful evidence to back up the theme of much of this book. There is a large body of uneducated, unqualified, ill-informed people who are offering expensive and incorrect advice to people about their lifestyle and diet. No apology is made if this appears offensive and hurtful because people in their ignorance are being taken advantage of. It is important of course to offer constructive advice to go with this criticism, so the following are the scientific and logical principles that need to be applied to lose and maintain weight loss.

1. Calorie Control.

A "normal" diet can be eaten. There is absolutely no need or reason to consume exotic, extreme, faddish or just plainly silly diets. What is important is that **FOOD SHOULD ONLY BE CONSUMED ON 3 OCCASIONS PER DAY.**

There is nothing wrong with consuming the "traditional" British high Calorie, high fat breakfast, but it would not be wise to consume it every day. The traditional roast British dinner is likewise perfectly healthy when allied to **Balance and Moderation.** What is not healthy and much harder to carry out in a balanced manner is the modern idea of "Grazing" and in between meal snacking. It is very much harder to maintain Calorie intake whilst the "snacks" tend to be high "empty" Calorie processed substances bearing little resemblance to "food". An important concept is that of "energy density" of food products. Snack foods tend to be high in both processed fat and carbohydrate and have energy densities of above 5 Calories/gram. Vegetables, fruit, salads and unrefined grains have energy densities of less than 1 Calorie/gram. The habit to consume low energy dense foods need to be developed from a young age, but unfortunately it is both cheaper and an easy option to consume high energy density foods.

2. Basal Metabolic Rate.

What a lazy bunch the developed world has become. Modern living has many advantages, but lack of exercise is not one of them. The previous narrative has shown that it is completely a waste of time dieting without changing the basal metabolic rate. **DIETING MAKES YOU FAT.** The game of rugby football has changed significantly in recent times and media viewing and interest in International games has increased. International, full-time rugby players consume huge numbers of Calories per day, but you no longer see over weight players. Many of them are very large physical specimens, but they are lean with it. They have high basal metabolic rates. A normal physiological adaptation to pregnancy is to lower the basal metabolic rate and so divert energy intake elsewhere. This surely, is the answer for maintained weight loss.

3. Bulky Food.

Obesity rates have increased with the growth of cheap, plentiful, palatable and pre-prepared processed food (?) coupled with the lack of exercise. These so called food products, by their very nature, are rapidly transported through the stomach and then absorbed by the small intestine. There is little, prolonged gastric extension and hence no feeling of **SATIETY.** The result is, following a highly processed meal or snack, feelings of hunger a short time after ingestion. This of course leads to renewed feeding of yet more high Calorie processed food products. Filling up on bulky carbohydrate and possibly protein enriched meals will induce a feeling of SATIETY whilst keeping the Calorie intake to an acceptable level.

At the beginning of this book reference was made to the fact that society had never had it so good whilst at the same time maybe there were aspects of the past, which were advantageous. Society in the developed world is presently sitting on a "time bomb" which will have enormous consequences. That "time bomb" is the problem of Obesity. This subject has a multi-factorial foundation of present day lifestyle allied to genetic disposition. There are people whose natural, genetic basal metabolic rate renders them unlikely to get over weight whereas other people will more readily become Obese. However, this genetic factor should not, as has been the case, be over-stated. Obesity does have a hormonal element, but again this only plays a very small part. As this book has attempted to show, the primary cause is most certainly **too many Calories and not enough exercise** and this I firmly believe is linked **to incorrect eating habits.** Those people who become over weight, whilst claiming the opposite, are almost certainly eating too many in between meal, high energy density snacks. The growth of pre-prepared processed food combined with the unacceptable supermarket practices have a lot to answer for.

The Central Council for Physical Recreation (CCPR) in Britain have recently made an announcement that for the first time a generation of children now have a life expectancy shorter than their parents.

Up to now this book has dealt with nothing but scientific facts. It has not been about my personal opinions but I should like to finish with a change of tense and give my opinions of present day lifestyle. I have been accused of being a bit of a dinosaur regarding how I view life and modern technology. I am happy with that. The computer is an abused and over-used machine, which is an impossible idea to grasp by the younger age groups who have grown up with it. The question of food production, retailing and consumption falls into a similar category. I am far from alone in my opinions regarding this as the growth in organic products, traditional sustainable farming and the slow food movements will confirm. I strongly believe we need to look backwards to a better time regarding the preparation and consumption of food. Eating is one of life's greatest pleasures and family meals **HAVE** to be retained. The great family occasions tend to take place around a dinner table and this important social event must continue. It was always my habit to frequent traditional greengrocers and butchers, and then to prepare and consume these raw ingredients. Whilst this is no longer quite the case due to the growing of home produce, raw ingredients are still daily prepared, cooked and then eaten. A frequent media topic is the loss of traditional crafts and services, and the butchers, bakers and green grocers are most certainly heading this way. The growth of supermarkets and their abhorrent practices does not bode well for the retention of proper raw ingredients. Like all of these services we either **use them or lose them.** Unfortunately, there is a severe problem to overcome, cooking. It appears we now have a society of non-cooks, because basic skills have already been lost and have not been passed on. Cooking basic, wholesome meals is straight forward if people are brought up correctly in preparing raw ingredients. Surely this is better than the household which has developed, with television sets in every bedroom, backed up with the latest computer technology and run on a cafeteria system of everyone eating different processed meals at different times. The fast food industry came up with a saying, which really has backfired, on them. There is no such thing as bad food, just bad diets. This is largely true but, **BALANCE AND MODERATION.** We should exist on properly prepared food, with no in between meal eating, but are allowed the so-called bad things occasionally. Hence, a full British cooked breakfast once a week or a restaurant fast food burger meal once a month are perfectly in order.

Some time ago I felt compelled to write a letter to the politicians in charge of health care in Britain. An absolutely vast sum of money is spent on the National Health Service (NHS) and a huge amount of this is wasted on unnecessary management costs. I pointed out that however much money was spent on the NHS it would never be enough because the system was inherently flawed. **There is no element of prevention within the NHS.** From my own personal experience and observation it became clear to me that the only way forward was to change the demand at the bottom end and reduce the need for treatment. This meant basically making the population healthier so they had less need to use the NHS. To this aim I suggested that a large, new body of workers was needed who would advise people on how to live a healthy lifestyle. The big problem was that although it is possible to teach these new workers the theory, it is not possible to imbue them with the necessary experience to make their role successful.

In 2004 a report was issued by a Professor Henry Becker on the problems facing Canada in supplying its health care needs. He pointed out the huge problems being faced due to degenerative conditions caused primarily by poor food intake practices and echoed my own thoughts concerning the problems in the NHS. It was also noted that the general medical practitioners are not sufficiently trained in dealing with the root cause of these degenerative conditions and do not have sufficient time. Prevention was not on the agenda.

**Obesity is a ticking time bomb
and change to Britain's dietary habits
must be made in a scientific and logical manner.**

SUGGESTED FURTHER READING

Silent Spring
Rachel Carson   ISBN 0 141 18494 9

The Language of the Genes
Steve Jones   ISBN 0 00 654676 5

The One-Straw Revolution
Masanobu Fukuoka   ISBN 81 85569 31 2

The Great Food Gamble
John Humphrys   ISBN 0 340 77045 7

So Shall We Reap
Colin Tudge   ISBN 0 141 00950 0

Don't Worry. Its Safe to Eat
Andrew Rowell   ISBN 1 85383 932 9

Not on the Label
Felicity Lawrence   ISBN 0 141 01566 7

Fast Food Nation
Eric Schlosser   ISBN 0 713 99602 1

APPENDIX

THE CURRENCY OF LIFE

adenosine

adenosine monophosphate (AMP)

adenosine diphosphate (ADP)

adenosine triphosphate (ATP)

MONOSACCHARIDES

CHO
|
HCOH
|
HOCH
|
HCOH
|
HOCH
|
CH₂OH

D-glucose

CHO
|
HCOH
|
HOCH
|
HOCH
|
HCOH
|
CH₂OH

D-galactose

CH₂OH
|
C=O
|
HOCH
|
HCOH
|
HCOH
|
CH₂OH

D-fructose

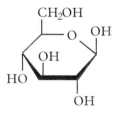

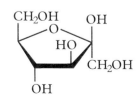

DISACCHARIDES

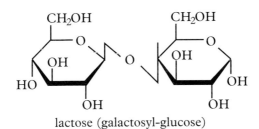

sucrose (glucosyl-fructose)

lactose (galactosyl-glucose)

maltose (glucosyl-glucose)

AMINO ACIDS

Amino acid	Symbol	R group	Amino acid	Symbol	R group
alanine	Ala	CH_3	leucine	Leu	CH_3 CH_3 CH CH_2
arginine	Arg	H_2N $C$$=NH$ NH $(CH_2)_3$	lysine	Lys	NH_2 $(CH_2)_4$
asparagine	Asn	$CONH_2$ CH_2	methionine	Met	CH_3 S $(CH_2)_2$
aspertic acid	Asn	COO^- CH_2			
cysteine	Cys	SH CH_2	phenylalanine	Phe	CH_2
glutamic acid	Glu	COO^- $(CH_2)_2$	proline (whole structure)	Pro	N $COOH$ H
glutamine	Gln	$CONH_2$ $(CH_2)_2$	serine	Ser	OH CH_2
glycine	Gly	H	threonine	Thr	OH $CH-CH_2$
histidine	His	HN N CH_2	tryptophan	Trp	H N CH_2
hydroxyproline (whole structure)	Hyp	HO $COOH$ N H	tyrosine	Tyr	OH CH_2
isoleucine	Ile	CH_3 $CH_2 CH_3$ CH	valine	Val	CH_3 CH_3 CH

FAT

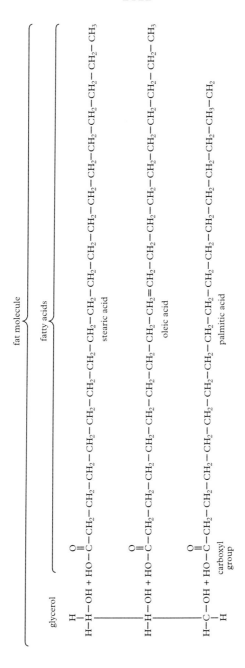

GLYCOLYSIS

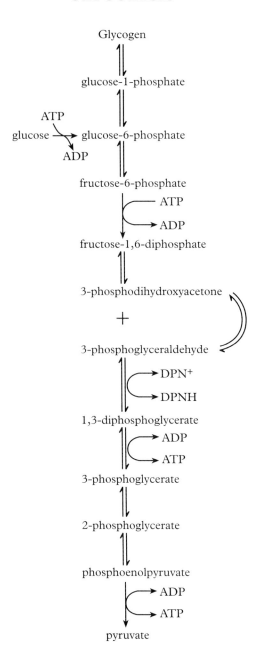

TCA CYCLE

Kerbs or Citric or Tricarboxylic Acid Cycle

This is where Glucose, Fat (Fatty acids), Protein (Amino acids) are finally processed. The Hydrogen (H) atoms which are released are then transported to the electron transport chain where, ATP is produced using the latent electro-chemical energy within the Hydrogen.

The Pyruvate, which is produced as the end product of GLYCOLYSIS, is converted to Acetyl CoA, which is also what happens to the chains of fatty acids. ie. 2 Carbon atoms out of the Fatty acid molecule are sequentially removed and converted to AcetylCoA.

Various Amino acids are able to insert themselves into varying positions of the Tricarboxylic cycle.

E-NUMBERS

Colours

E100	Curcumin
E101(i)	Riboflavin
E101(ii)	Riboflavin-5'-phosphate
E102	Tartrazine
E104	Quinoline yellow
E110	Sunset Yellow FCF; Orange Yellow S
E120	Cochineal; Carminic acid; Carmines
E122	Azorubine; Carmoisine
E123	Amaranth
E124	Ponceau 4R; Cochineal Red A
E127	Erythrosine
E128	Red 2G
E129	Allura Red AC
E131	Patent Blue V
E132	Indigotine; Indigo Carmine
E133	Brilliant Blue FCF
E140	Chlorophylls and chlorophyllins
E141	Copper complexes of chlorophyll and chlorophyllins
E142	Green S
E150a	Plain caramel
E150b	Caustic sulphite caramel
E150c	Ammonia caramel
E150d	Sulphite ammonia caramel
E151	Brilliant Black BN; Black PN
E153	Vegetable carbon
E154	Brown FK
E155	Brown HT
E160a	Carotenes
E160b	Annatto; Bixin; Norbixin
E160c	Paprika extract; Capsanthian; Capsorubin
E160d	Lycopene
E160e	Beta-apo-8'-carotenal (C30)
E160f	Ethyl ester of beta-apo-8'-carotenoic acid (C30)
E161b	Lutein
E161g	Canthaxanthin
E162	Beetroot Red; Betanin
E163	Anthocyanins
E170	Calcium carbonate
E171	Titanium dioxide
E172	Iron oxides and hydroxides
E173	Aluminium
E174	Silver
E175	Gold
E180	Litholrubine BK

Preservatives

E200	Sorbic acid
E202	Potassium sorbate
E203	Calcium sorbate
E210	Benzoic acid
E211	Sodium benzoate
E212	Potassium benzoate
E213	Calcium benzoate
E214	Ethyl p-hydroxybenzoate
E215	Sodium ethyl p-hydroxybenzoate
E216	Propyl p-hydroxybenzoate
E217	Sodium propyl p-hydroxybenzoate
E218	Methyl p-hydroxybenzoate
E219	Sodium methyl p-hydroxybenzoate
E220	Sulphur dioxide
E221	Sodium sulphite
E222	Sodium hydrogen sulphite
E223	Sodium metabisuiphite
E224	Potassium metabisulphite
E226	Calcium sulphite
E227	Calcium hydrogen sulphite
E228	Potassium hydrogen sulphite
E230	Biphenyl; diphenyl
E231	Orthophenyl phenol
E232	Sodium orthophenyl phenol
E234	Nisin
E235	Natamycin
E239	Hexamethylene tetramine
E242	Dimethyl dicarbonate
E249	Potassium nitrite
E250	Sodium nitrite
E251	Sodium nitrate
E252	Potassium nitrate
E280	Propionic acid
E281	Sodium propionate
E282	Calcium propionate
E283	Potassium propionate
E284	Boric acid
E285	Sodium tetraborate; borax
E1105	Lysozyme

Antioxidants

E300	Ascorbic acid
E301	Sodium ascorbate
E302	Calcium ascorbate
E304	Fatty acid esters of ascorbic acid
E306	Tocopherols
E307	Alpha-tocopherol
E308	Gamma-tocopherol
E309	Delta-tocopherol
E310	Propyl gallate
E311	Octyl gallate
E312	Dodecyl gallate
E315	Erythorbic acid
E316	Sodium erythorbate
E320	Butylated hydroxyanisole (BHA)
E321	Butylated hydroxytoluene (BHT)

Sweeteners

E420(i)	Sorbitol
E420(ii)	Sorbitol syrup
E421	Mannitol
E953	Isomalt
E965(i)	Maltitol
E965(ii)	Maltitol syrup
E966	Lactitol
E967	Xylitol
E950	Acesulfame K
E951	Aspartame
E952	Cyclamic acid and its Na and Ca salts
E954	Saccharin and its Na, K and Ca salts
E957	Thaumatin
E959	Neohesperidine DC

Emulsifiers, Stabilisers, Thickeners and Gelling Agents

E322	Lecithins
E400	Alginic acid
E401	Sodium alginate
E402	Potassium alginate
E403	Ammonium alginate
E404	Calcium alginate
E405	Propane-1,2-diol alginate
E406	Agar
E407	Carrageenan
E407a	Processed eucheuma seaweed
E410	Locust bean gum; carob gum
E412	Guar gum
E413	Tragacanth
E414	Acacia gum; gum arabic
E415	Xanthan gum
E416	Karaya gum
E417	Tara gum
E418	Gellan gum
E425	Konjac
E432	Polyoxyethylene sorbitan monolaurate; Polysorbate 20
E433	Polyoxyethylene sorbitan mono-oleate; Polysorbate 80
E434	Polyoxyethylene sorbitan monopalmitate; Polysorbate 40
E435	Polyoxyethylene sorbitan monostearate; Polysorbate 60
E436	Polyoxyethylene sorbitan tristearate; Polysorbate 65
E440	Pectins
E442	Ammonium phosphatides
E444	Sucrose acetate isobutyrate
E445	Glycerol esters of wood rosins
E460	Cellulose
E461	Methyl cellulose
E463	Hydroxypropyl cellulose
E464	Hydroxypropyl methyl cellulose
E465	Ethyl methyl cellulose
E466	Carboxy methyl cellulose
E467	Sodium carboxy methyl cellulose
E468	Crosslinked sodium carboxy methyl cellulose
E469	Enzymatically hydrolysed carboxy methyl cellulose
E470a	Sodium, potassium and calcium salts of fatty Acids
E470b	Magnesium salts of fatty acids
E471	Mono- and diglycerides of fatty acids
E472a	Acetic acid esters of mono- and diglycerides of fatty acids
E472b	Lactic acid esters of mono- and diglycerides of fatty acids
E472c	Citric acid esters of mono- and diglycerides of fatty acids
E472d	Tartaric acid esters of mono- and diglycerides of fatty acids

E472e	Mono- and diacetyltartaric acid esters of mono- and diglycerides of fatty acids	E333	Calcium citrates
		E334	Tartaric acid (L-(+))
		E335	Sodium tartrates
E472f	Mixed acetic and tartaric acid esters of mono- and diglycerides of fatty acids	E336	Potassium tartrates
		E337	Sodium potassium tartrate
		E338	Phosphoric acid
E473	Sucrose esters of fatty acids	E339	Sodium phosphates
E474	Sucroglycerides	E340	Potassium phosphates
E475	Polyglycerol esters of fatty acids	E341	Calcium phosphates
		E343	Magnesium phosphates
E476	Polyglycerol polyricinoleate	E350	Sodium malates
E477	Propane-1,2-diol esters of fatty acids	E351	Potassium malate
		E352	Calcium malates
E479b	Thermally oxidised soya bean oil interacted with mono and diglycerides of fatty acids	E353	Metatartaric acid
		E354	Calcium tartrate
		E355	Adipic acid
E481	Sodium stearoyl-2-lactylate	E356	Sodium adipate
E482	Calcium stearoyl-2-lactylate	E357	Potassium adipate
E483	Stearyl tartrate	E363	Succinic acid
E491	Sorbitan monostearate	E380	Triammonium citrate
E492	Sorbitan tristearate	E385	Calcium disodium ethylene diamine tetra-acetate; calcium disodium EDTA
E493	Sorbitan monolaurate		
E494	Sorbitan monooleate		
E495	Sorbitan monopalmitate	E422	Glycerol
E1103	Invertase	E431	Polyoxyethylene (40) stearate

Others

Acid, acidity regulators, anti-caking agents, anti-foaming agents, bulking agents, carriers and carriersolvents, emulsifying salts, firming agents, flavour enhancers, flour treatment agents, foaming agents, glazing agents, humectants, modified starches, packaging gases, propellants, raising agents andsequestrants.

		E450	Diphosphates
		E451	Triphosphates
		E452	Polyphosphates
		E459	Beta-cyclodextrin
		E500	Sodium carbonates
		E501	Potassium carbonates
		E503	Ammonium carbonates
		E504	Magnesium carbonates
		E507	Hydrochloric acid
		E508	Potassium chloride
E170	Calcium carbonates	E509	Calcium chloride
E260	Acetic acid	E511	Magnesium chloride
E261	Potassium acetate	E512	Stannous chloride
E262	Sodium acetate	E513	Sulphuric acid
E263	Calcium acetate	E514	Sodium sulphates
E270	Lactic acid	E515	Potassium sulphates
E290	Carbon dioxide	E516	Calcium sulphate
E296	Malic acid	E517	Ammonium sulphate
E297	Fumaric acid	E520	Aluminium sulphate
E325	Sodium lactate	E521	Aluminium sodium sulphate
E326	Potassium lactate	E522	Aluminium potassium sulphate
E327	Calcium lactate		
E330	Citric acid	E523	Aluminium ammonium sulphate
E331	Sodium citrates		
E332	Potassium citrates	E524	Sodium hydroxide

E525	Potassium hydroxide	E904	Shellac
E526	Calcium hydroxide	E905	Microcrystalline wax
E527	Ammonium hydroxide	E912	Montan acid esters
E528	Magnesium hydroxide	E914	Oxidised Polyethylene wax
E529	Calcium oxide	E920	L-Cysteine
E530	Magnesium oxide	E927b	Carbamide
E535	Sodium ferrocyanide	E938	Argon
E536	Potassium ferrocyanide	E939	Helium
E538	Calcium ferrocyanide	E941	Nitrogen
E541	Sodium aluminium phosphate	E942	Nitrous oxide
E551	Silicon dioxide	E943a	Butane
E 552	Calcium silicate	E943b	Iso-butane
E553a(i)	Magnesium silicate	E944	Propane
E553a(ii)	Magnesium trisilicate	E948	Oxygen
E553b	Talc	E949	Hydrogen
E554	Sodium aluminium silicate	E999	Quillaia extract
E555	Potassium aluminium silicate	E1200	Polydextrose
E556	Aluminium calcium silicate	E1201	Polyvinylpyrrolidone
E558	Bentonite	E1202	Polyvinylpolypyrrolidone
E559	Aluminium silicate; Kaolin	E1404	Oxidised starch
E570	Fatty acids	E1410	Monostarch phosphate
E574	Gluconic acid	E1412	Distarch phosphate
E575	Glucono delta-lactone	E1413	Phosphated distarch phosphate
E576	Sodium gluconate	E1414	Acetylated starch
E577	Potassium gluconate	E1420	Acetylated Starch
E578	Calcium gluconate	E1422	Acetylated distarch adipate
E579	Ferrous gluconate	E1440	Hydroxyl propyl starch
E585	Ferrous lactate	E1442	Hydroxy propyl distarch
E620	Glutamic acid		phosphate
E621	Monosodium glutamate	E1450	Starch sodium octenyl
E622	Monopotassium glutamate		succinate
E623	Calcium diglutamate	E1451	Acetylated oxidised starch
E624	Monoammonium glutamate		Polyethylene glycol 6000
E625	Magnesium diglutamate	E1505	Triethyl citrate
E626	Guanylic acid	E1518	Glyceryl triacetate; triacetin
E627	Disodium guanylate	E1520	Propan-1,2-diol; propylene
E628	Dipotassium guanylate		glycol
E629	Calcium guanylate		
E630	lnosinic acid		
E631	Disodium inosinate		
E632	Dipotassium inosinate		
E633	Calcium inosinate		
E634	Calcium 5'-ribonucleotides		
E635	Disodium 5'-ribonucieotides		
E640	Glycine and its sodium salt		
E650	Zinc acetate		
E900	Dimethylpolysiloxane		
E901	Beeswax, white and yellow		
E902	Candelilla wax		
E903	Carnauba wax		

About the Author

Anthony Smith B.D.S. B.Sc.

Anthony Smith qualified as a Dentist in 1978 and moved into general dental practice in Oxford. After an initial settling in period he began to look at his patients' mouths more critically and question the destructive effect of their diet. The logical next step was to question the role of diet on the whole body and so began the process of investigating food production and the environment. He began to think about growing his own produce in order to have more control over what he ate.

In 1986 Anthony Smith moved to Lincoln where he opened a new dental practice and bought a run down property, which had an allotment-sized garden. He started growing his own fruit and vegetables and became aware of HDRA, which was the leading organic gardening organisation. During the rest of the 1980's he became more conscious of poor food production practices, especially meat, and the problems of environmental pollution. During the early 1990's he continued to gain knowledge in vegetable growing and became self-sufficient in organically grown fruit and vegetables. His business developed with him opening a second dental practice nearer his home. Like many other members of the dental profession, Anthony Smith was affected by increasing time constraint problems and in order to maintain standards was forced to alter his working arrangements and convert his dental practice to the private sector. This eventually led to the sale of his first Lincoln dental practice and all his time being devoted to a smaller number of patients at his second practice. A big change of emphasis ensued with his dental practice now highly geared towards prevention and being able to use his experience to advise patients on good dietary practice. On a number of occasions patients suggest that Anthony Smith should write a book.

In Autumn 1996, Anthony Smith enrolled at Riseholme College, Lincoln for a Royal Horticulture Society Diploma evening course to learn more about plants. In 1998 he enrolled with the Open University and in 2001 gained an upper second B.Sc. honours degree in Biological Natural Science. Following this he returned to Riseholme College with a view to doing a Ph.D into the role of Vitamin C in Blackcurrants but a change to the College stalled this. However, having acquired some basic computer skills, further research is still possible via the Internet. During 2003, due to the poor dietary health and advice exhibited in the United Kingdom, his hand is forced and he writes a book (this is that book).

Along the way Anthony Smith has joined HDRA and the heritage seed library, Compassion in World Farming, Friends of the Earth, International Society for Horticultural Science, Pesticide Action Network (UK) and The Food Commission. He is currently undertaking a Master of Medical Science degree in Human Nutrition at Sheffield University so that he can formalise and increase the knowledge he has gained over the last 25 years.

NOTES